CAREERS
IN ADVERTISING

VGM Professional Careers Series

CAREERS
IN ADVERTISING

S. WILLIAM PATTIS

Foreword by
Jarlath J. (Jack) Graham
Former Editor
Advertising Age

VGM Career Horizons
a division of *NTC Publishing Group*
Lincolnwood, Illinois USA

Library of Congress Cataloging-in-Publication Data

Pattis, S. William.
  Careers in advertising / S. William Pattis.

      p. cm. — (VGM professional careers series)
    ISBN 0-8442-8696-6 : $14.95. — ISBN 0-8442-8697-4 (pbk.) : $9.95
    1. Advertising—Vocational guidance. I. Title. II. Series.
  HF5827.P378 1990   90-12135
  659.1'023'73—dc20   CIP

Published by VGM Career Horizons, a division of NTC Publishing Group.
© 1990 by NTC Publishing Group, 4255 West Touhy Avenue,
Lincolnwood (Chicago), Illinois 60646-1975 U.S.A.
Manufactured in the United States of America.

0 1 2 3 4 5 6 7 8 9 ML 9 8 7 6 5 4 3 2 1

CONTENTS

ABOUT THE AUTHOR

S. William "Bill" Pattis likes to tell people how he started his lifetime career in publishing and advertising in 1933 when at the age of eight he sold the *Saturday Evening Post* for a nickel a copy to commuters at the neighborhood train station in Chicago's Hyde Park community. At twelve, he was a co-owner of a corner newsstand.

His career came to a standstill for the next nine years as he finished high school, served in Europe as a combat engineer during World War II, and completed his studies obtaining a degree in Marketing and Management at the University of Illinois in 1949. While in college, he was heavily involved in extracurricular activities that contributed much to his flair for advertising and promotion.

His first post-college job was in Chicago selling advertising for United Business Publications at $40 per week. In the evenings, he continued his studies in the graduate school at Northwestern University. He progressed rapidly and at age 29 was moved to New York by his employer to become publisher of *Photographic Trade News*. In quick succession, his responsibilities were expanded to assume the full publishing responsibilities for five magazines.

At age 33, he returned to Chicago to establish The Pattis Group, which he headed as Chairman and Chief Executive Officer. Under his direction the firm became the world's largest in magazine advertising sales, with offices in Chicago, New York, Los Angeles, Atlanta, Miami, Honolulu, Toronto, London and Paris. The firm is now Pattis/3M and functions as an operating division of the Advertising Services Group of the giant 3M Company. In this work the author was involved on a daily basis with most national advertisers and probably all of the advertising agencies in America; the scope of these activities has formed the basis for much of the knowledge and information found in this book.

The author's writings include many articles that have appeared in the advertising press and two other books on advertising and media. His speaking engagements have included appearances before The National Association of Publishers Representatives, The Overseas Press and Media Association, and the International Media Buyers' Association. He participated in the first Face-to-Face International conference in The Hague, Netherlands, and has been a principal speaker at the annual meeting of the Periodical Publishers Association of the United Kingdom. In 1988 he participated in the first U.S.-U.S.S.R. bilateral talks in Moscow involving members of American media and their Soviet counterparts.

As is typical for many people in communications, he has served on various civic and charitable committees throughout his business life. In the late '60s and early '70s, he received commendations from both Vice-Presidents Humphrey and Agnew for his work on the President's Council for Youth Opportunity. Presently he serves as Chairman of the Book and Library Committee of the United States Information Agency and is on the Executive Committee of the Publishing Hall of Fame.

His other business interests include directorships of two banks, President of P-B Communications, publisher of Chicago's *North Shore* magazine, trustee of Eisenhower Medical Center in Rancho Mirage, California, and President of NTC Publishing Group, publisher of the VGM Career Horizons Books.

ACKNOWLEDGMENTS

For whatever reason you picked up this book, you obviously have an interest in advertising...good for you! If that interest is to seek a career, then read on, because you have chosen a dynamic profession that demands the best in one's creativity, along with hard work, upredictable hours, the ability to ride the crest of success and also to be able to handle the frustration of defeat. You will find it all in advertising, and if you are really good, you'll enjoy the work and also probably make a pile of money.

Having spent over 40 years in the fast-paced world of advertising and publishing, my family has had to share it all. Therefore, I would like to dedicate this book to my one and only wife of 40 years, Bette, my adult children and their spouses, Mark and Anne-Françoise Pattis of Evanston, Illinois, and Robin and Roger Himovitz of Montecito, California. Also, a special mention of my two wonderful grandchildren, Rachael and Benjamin Himovitz, with the hope that this book will give them a little more by which to remember "Popi" in the years to come.

Finally, I owe a very special thanks to Jeffrey S. Johnson for his splendid research and help in the assembling of this book.

FOREWORD

Advertising is an essential force in today's marketplace. It serves sellers by convincing people to buy their products or services and serves consumers by providing information on what's available in the marketplace. But advertising is more complex than just a copywriter and an artist working together to produce ads.

Ad people must determine who they must reach with their sales message and what media will most effectively target the appropriate audience. As domestic and foreign competition grow in intensity, the demand for mature, creative, hard-working advertising professionals will increase.

Young people hear primarily about advertising agencies, and perhaps they should because that's where most advertising is created. However, few realize the wide range of advertising career possibilities that are associated with agency jobs. One of the aspects of advertising often overlooked is media sales—an area that the author of this book knows from the ground up. Also often overlooked is the promise of rewarding careers in the advertising departments of advertiser companies.

This book covers the entire advertising industry and the broad range of career possibilities that are available. There is a wealth of information on careers in creative services, account services, media services, research, print production, traffic, agency management, brand management and media sales. Even careers related to advertising, such as public relations, publicity, sales promotion and direct mail, are covered. Top ad agencies and advertisers in terms of billings and expenditures are identified in the numerous tables that appear throughout the book.

Is advertising for you? What are the career possibilities in advertising? With this book, Bill Pattis helps you get answers. You'll find useful information on how agencies work, what types of jobs are available, how to get the proper education and training, and a look at current salary levels. And you'll see that there are needs for talented writers, artists, and people with many other skills in the vast world of advertising. Good luck in your career endeavors!

Jarlath J. (Jack) Graham
Former Editor
Advertising Age

ADVERTISING: YESTERDAY AND TODAY

From ancient times down to the present, advertising has played an important role in society. It is indispensable in our modern society, simply because it helps to inform the public of the basic goods and services that are available in today's marketplace. Advertising can be defined as any form of paid communication that is intended to motivate a reader or viewer to purchase a product or a service, to influence public opinion, to win political support, to sell an idea or a cause, or to act or think and perhaps influence others in a manner desired by the advertiser. As one can see, there are many purposes for advertising, but the main goal is to motivate or persuade people to buy a particular product or service. Advertisers use such media as radio, television, newspapers, magazines, direct mail, billboards, posters, catalogs, and brochures to persuade the public to buy products, to vote for people, to believe in a particular cause, or to accept a certain idea. Whether they are promoting a product or an idea, advertisers are in the business of selling.

Unlike other forms of communication, such as editorial and news reporting, feature articles in magazines, and news and entertainment on radio and television, advertising is paid for by the advertiser, who, in turn, has control of what the public hears or sees, subject only to conditions set forth by the media carrying the message. The advertiser knows that the message will appear exactly as intended. On the other hand, advertisers generally take care to be sure that their advertising is truthful and does not mislead the public.

The advertiser and the advertising agency decide the form of an advertisement and what medium is best to promote the product or service. Most media depend on advertising for all or the major portion of their revenues. The majority of television and radio programs are funded by advertising revenue, and a large number of newspapers and magazines depend on advertising to absorb their costs and to generate a profit.

Without advertising, there is little need for billboards, posters, and most catalogs. Advertising's importance to the communications industry is immeasurable. In fact, most of the media that we take for granted would be extremely expensive to the reader or viewer or would be out of business without the revenues produced by advertising.

Advertising can be a rewarding and challenging profession. Those considering a career in the field of advertising should be encouraged by the continued growth the industry has experienced in recent years and by the constant need for fresh, young talent.

THE EVOLUTION OF ADVERTISING

In order to understand how advertising has grown to its current level of influence and importance, one needs to understand the history and development of the industry through the centuries. Many people seem to think that advertising is a relatively new field, an industry that has only recently become a force in the economy. Nothing could be further from the truth. Advertising, in one form or another, has been going on since ancient times.

Probably the earliest existing example of advertising in its original form is housed in the British Museum in London. It consists of a sheet of papyrus that bears a notice of a runaway slave and a reward for his return. This advertisement was found in Egypt and is more than 3,000 years old.

As early as 3000 B.C. Babylonian merchants hired barkers to shout their wares to passersby. Signs employed by tradespeople to state the nature of their business were found in the ruins of Babylon. Since few people could read, these signs carried illustrations of the product or service offered: a loaf of bread for a bakery, a boot for a shoemaker's shop. In Greece, town criers were sometimes accompanied by musicians, and in ancient Egypt, town criers told of the arrival of ships with new merchandise.

The invention of the printing press in the fifteenth century brought with it the start of the advertising evolution. Almost as soon as the presses were rolling they were being used for advertising. The earliest printed advertisements were handbills and announcements bound into books. A handbill would usually show the sign that hung over the door of the shop and include brief copy underneath in script.

In the seventeenth century, the public press arrived and enticed businesses into selling their wares through the printed page on a grander scale. Soon, commercial notices were inserted with other news items. In England, for example, tea, coffee, and chocolate served at various pubs throughout the country were advertised. In 1660 King Charles II advertised the loss of a few royal pets. Directories containing only advertising were published. Finally, with the publication of the first English daily newspaper, the London *Daily Courant* (1702), advertising began to prosper both in quantity and quality.

In the United States advertising has been commonplace since the Revolutionary War. Like most newspapers of its day, the *Pennsylvania Packet and Daily Advertiser,* in which the Constitution of the United States was first published, carried advertising for goods that had just arrived from abroad. It also published ships' sailing notices and alerted the public to the services of tailors, cobblers, candlestick makers, and other tradespeople of the era. Most of this advertising was meant to inform, although there was some competitive persuasion in the advertisements for millinery and rum. Printed pamphlets and broadsides were used to sway the dissatisfied American colonists toward revolution.

From that time to the middle of the nineteenth century, merchants wrote and placed their own advertising in local magazines and newspapers. As the country grew and transportation, communication, and distribution systems improved, many businesses were eager to expand their sales into broader markets. The result was that the publishers of newspapers and other periodicals hired advertising agents to help sell the advertising to retailers and manufacturers. The agents acted as liaisons between publisher and advertiser, and the ads were usually prepared by the advertiser or the advertising agent. These agents functioned as the first advertising agencies. In some cases agents were employed and paid by the publishers, not by the advertisers. Other so-called agents were merely brokers of space—that is, they would negotiate to buy space in a newspaper at a favorable rate and then sell the space to one or more advertisers for whatever price they could get. As a result of these tactics, which were often questionable, advertising agents earned unsavory reputations.

Then in the late 1860's, a man by the name of N.W. Ayer changed the whole advertising system. Ayer determined it would be better to represent the interests of the advertisers rather than the publishers. He hired writers, artists, and other creative people and convinced the advertisers that his firm could create advertising that would produce better results. With his new approach, Ayer began to bring some order to the advertising business, and in doing so, he brought a measure of respectability to the profession as well. The modern advertising agency was born.

From this beginning, all the present-day advertising services developed. Advertising agents and others began to produce the advertising for their clients. Most important the advertiser expected the agent to produce ads that brought measurable results.

By 1870 the use of magazines for general advertising became a common practice. Advertising allowed magazines to increase their circulation as they reduced their cover price. By the turn of the century, major magazines, such as *McClure's* and *Cosmopolitan* carried more than 100 pages of ads in each issue. Advertising expenditures in the United States rose from $60 million in 1867 to $360 million in 1890.

Technological innovations fueled the remarkable growth of the advertising industry in the late nineteenth century. These accomplishments included the invention of the rotary press in 1849, the manufacture of paper from wood pulp in 1866, the introduction of the linotype in 1884, and half-tone engraving in 1893.

THE TWENTIETH CENTURY AND MEDIA DEVELOPMENT

The twentieth century brought with it many major technological breakthroughs in the communications field that resulted in a direct impact on the advertising industry.

At the end of the nineteenth century, advertisers had a limited choice of media available to them. Besides daily newspapers and magazines, there were handbills, hand-painted signs, and billboards. And except for signs, there was not much opportunity to use color in advertisements. Colored paper stock and ink existed, but due to high costs and limited supply, very little use was made of either. Consequently, what the public read were black-and-white advertisements accompanied by fairly unappealing illustrations and as much copy as possible. With a few exceptions, advertising of that period was extremely cluttered and unprofessional compared to today's standards. Its unattractiveness made it easy to ignore.

As time passed, though, technology was developed to print magazines with color, followed by the perfection of four-color rotogravure sections for Sunday newspapers. Rotogravure made it possible to print full color on a rotary press, and it was accomplished faster and for less expense.

Design principles also began to improve, and advertisements began to focus on one product instead of showing many different products. Advertising became more arresting and attractive, and people's attention, interest, and response were heightened.

The growth of radio in the 1920s brought with it a new advertising medium and new opportunities for the industry. By 1928 commercial radio accounted for $10.5 million in advertising. These first radio programs were followed in the 1930s and 1940s by network programs starring such popular celebrities as Eddie Cantor, Fred Allen, George Burns, and Jack Benny. It was during this period that the effectiveness of using celebrities to endorse products became popular. With the advent of radio, advertising began to enter people's homes for the entire family to hear, and this increased the pervasiveness of advertising and deepened its influence on people of all ages and life-styles.

Commercial radio made it possible for national advertisers to reach large numbers of people and expand market coverage. Many products sponsored entire shows, such as the Jello Program and the Lux Radio Theatre, which developed huge devoted audiences. When a product was associated with a popular radio show, it enhanced the company's image and sales.

Of course the single most important development of the century in communications and advertising was television. Television opened up great possibilities for advertisers. The ability to reach millions of households with a visual image led to unprecedented growth in the advertising industry. No longer were advertising agencies restricted to the use of words and still pictures to sell products—they now could add action to their message.

In the beginning, most advertisers and their agencies felt that TV would be useful and valuable, but few had any idea of what an enormously powerful force this medium would become. It was commonplace in the early days to hear that television was a combination of sounds and words and pictures, and that it would add a new dimension to radio and print media, but TV's unique power was grossly underestimated. It is apparent today, of course, that television has multiplied advertising's exposure immeasurably. In spite of the early uncertainty, by 1955 advertisers were spending over $1 billion a year on television advertising. By the late 1960s there were over fifty-eight million homes with television sets and over six hundred broadcasting stations.

As a matter of interest, two examples attest to the tremendous impact of television. For one, the magazine with the nation's largest circulation is *TV Guide,* the content of which deals exclusively with television. For another, a thirty-second commercial on prime-time TV—which costs anywhere from $50,000 up to $500,000—may be seen by 50 million people at the exact same time. Special events, such as the Super Bowl, are seen by as many as 100 million people.

Today cable television is adding another lucrative dimension to television advertising. Cable technology not only allows viewers to see TV commercials in a traditional manner, but it now enables consumers to purchase products by phone or through the use of home computerized purchasing systems. As communication technology has advanced, so has advertising continued to advance and to provide new and exciting ways to inform people about products and services.

ADVERTISING CODES AND REGULATIONS

The various laws, codes, regulations, and principles imposed by the government on advertisers are aimed at protecting the public from fraudulent and misleading advertising claims. Due to these restrictions, the frequency of misleading or false advertising has significantly dwindled in recent years.

The Federal Trade Commission (FTC) monitors advertising in the United States to determine whether it is false or misleading. The FTC may require advertisers to provide proof of their claims or may order advertisers to remove advertisements that are considered questionable. Specific types of advertising are regulated by other government agencies.

It is fair to assume that each of these government agencies is dedicated to what it believes to be the public welfare and, therefore, sees itself on the side of "right." What makes life complicated for the advertising practitioner, however, is that there are frequent disagreements among these organizations, making it hard to determine which concept of "right" is more valid at a given time.

No doubt a reasonable consensus will be reached in due course, but until such time, advertising people will have to be sensitive to the fact that there are many conflicting signals.

This century has also seen a rising social consciousness that has led to the establishment of voluntary associations operating under self-imposed regulations designed to discourage and penalize improper or unethical practices. The American Association of Advertising Agencies (AAAA) is one such group; the Association of National Advertisers is another. The National Association of Broadcasters also has a strict code that applies to what may or may not be aired on television or radio. In the field of magazine publishing, there are such groups as the Magazine Publishers Association and the American Association of Business Publishers. Newspaper publishers also have set standards of what is acceptable advertising for their newspapers.

A new regulatory group is the National Advertising Division (NAD), which was formed by advertisers, agencies, and the National Better Business Bureau to review complaints about false or misleading advertising. The NAD investigates complaints and attempts to work out settlements so that all parties involved are satisfied. If no settlement can be reached, an appeal is made to the National Advertising Review Board, a five-member body with representatives from advertising and the public sector. The board has the power to cause advertising that it considers questionable to be discontinued or amended.

Despite the regulatory groups, there are still abuses and occasional misleading claims in advertising. But such claims are becoming more infrequent. It may be fair to say that some of today's advertising is considered to be objectionable due to poor taste rather than to any actual fraudulence. Since taste is subjective, it seems probable that this condition will continue; so far, no formula for imposing uniform standards of taste has been discovered, nor is this likely to occur in the future.

The self-imposed code of the American Advertising Federation reads as follows:

The Advertising Code of American Business

1. *Truth*...Advertising shall tell the truth, and shall reveal significant facts, the concealment of which would mislead the public.
2. *Responsibility*...Advertising agencies and advertisers shall be willing to provide substantiation of claims made.

3. *Taste and Decency*...Advertising shall be free of statements, illustrations, or implications which are offensive to good taste or public decency.

4. *Bait Advertising*...Advertising shall offer only merchandise or services which are readily available for purchase at the advertised price.

5. *Guarantees and Warranties*...Advertising of guarantees and warranties shall be explicit. Advertising of any guarantee or warranty shall clearly and conspicuously disclose its nature and extent, the manner in which the guarantor or warrantor will perform, and the identity of the guarantor or warrantor.

6. *Price Claims*...Advertising shall avoid price or savings claims which are false or misleading, or which do not offer provable bargains or savings.

7. *Unprovable Claims*...Advertising shall avoid the use of exaggerated or unprovable claims.

8. *Testimonials*...Advertising containing testimonials shall be limited to those of competent witnesses who are reflecting a real and honest choice.

Creative Code
American Association of Advertising Agencies

The members of the American Association of Advertising Agencies recognize:

1. That advertising bears a dual responsibility in the American economic system and way of life.

To the public it is a primary way of knowing about the goods and services which are the products of American free enterprise, goods and services which can be freely chosen to suit the desires and needs of the individual. The public is entitled to expect that advertising will be reliable in content and honest in presentation.

To the advertiser it is a primary way of persuading people to buy his goods or services, within the framework of a highly competitive economic system. He is entitled to regard advertising as a dynamic means of building his business and his profits.

2. That advertising enjoys a particularly intimate relationship to the American family. It enters the home as an integral part of television and radio programs, to speak to the individual and often to the entire family. It shares the pages of favorite newspapers and magazines. It presents itself to travelers and to readers of the daily mails. In all these forms, it bears a special responsibility to respect the tastes and self-interest of the public.

3. That advertising is directed to sizable groups or to the public at large, which is made up of many interests and many tastes. As is the case with all public enterprises, ranging from sports to education and even to religion, it is almost impossible to speak without finding someone in disagreement. Nonetheless, advertising people recognize their obligation to operate within the traditional American limitations: to serve the interests of the majority and to respect the rights of the minority.

Therefore we, the members of the American Association of Advertising Agencies, in addition to supporting and obeying the laws and legal regulations pertaining to advertising, undertake to extend and broaden the application of high ethical standards. Specifically, we will not knowingly produce advertising which contains:

- a. False or misleading statements or exaggerations, visual or verbal.
- b. Testimonials which do not reflect the real choice of a competent witness.
- c. Price claims which are misleading.
- d. Comparisons which unfairly disparage a competitive product or service.
- e. Claims insufficiently supported, or which distort the true meaning or practicable application of statements made by professional or scientific authority.
- f. Statements, suggestions, or pictures offensive to public decency.

We recognize that there are areas which are subject to honestly different interpretations and judgment. Taste is subjective and may even vary from time to time as well as from individual to individual. Frequency of seeing or hearing advertising messages will necessarily vary greatly from person to person.

However, we agree not to recommend to an advertiser and to discourage the use of advertising which is in poor or questionable taste or which is deliberately irritating through content, presentation, or excessive repetition.

Clear and willful violations of this Code shall be referred to the Board of Directors of the American Association of Advertising Agencies for appropriate action, including possible annulment of membership as provided in Article IV, Section 5, of the Constitution and By-Laws.

Conscientious adherence to the letter and the spirit of this Code will strengthen advertising and the free enterprise system of which it is part.

Adopted April 26, 1962

Endorsed by Advertising Association of the West, Advertising Federation of America, Agricultural Publishers Association, Associated Business Publications, Association of Industrial Advertisers, Association of National Advertisers, Magazine Publishers Association, National Business Publications, Newspaper Advertising Executives Association, Radio Code Review Board (National Association of Broadcasters), Station Representatives Association, TV Code Review Board (NAP).

ADVERTISING AND PUBLIC CAUSES

Many advertisers, advertising agencies, and media companies join each year in donating large amounts of time, energy, money, space, and air time to public causes. Most of these efforts are administered by an organization called The Advertising Council, which has been serving worthy causes for over forty years. It is a private, nonprofit organization, supported exclusively by the advertising and communications industries and by American business. The Advertising Council works hand-in-hand with the American Association of Advertising Agencies in its efforts to promote causes for the public good. These projects are aimed at increasing public interest in worthy causes that could not normally afford to pay for costly advertising.

The operating budget of the Council, contributed by the member companies, is close to $1.9 million a year; a recent estimate of the value of the space and time donated by the media every year totals over $1 billion. Specific projects are assigned to individual agencies, which develop the campaign at their own expense.

Some of the causes supported by the Advertising Council include the following:

- AIDS awareness
- Aid to higher education
- Alcoholism prevention
- American Red Cross
- Child abuse prevention
- Drug abuse prevention
- Forest fire prevention
- Help prevent crime
- Peace Corps
- Take Pride in America/Protect Your Public Lands
- United Negro College Fund
- United Way

There are many charities, social service agencies, and educational institutions that use advertising to educate people about health problems or to solicit contributions for research activities. On any given week, one will see a number of these appeals, often made by well-known celebrities.

Almost every major advertising agency along with many advertisers have a few pet charitable, civic, or educational projects that they support at their own expense and by actively lobbying for the support of members of the media. There is no way of knowing how much money is contributed in this fashion, but a conservative estimate would be that approximately $300 million is invested annually in these activities.

It is clear that advertising is a useful and necessary part of our modern society, and that much of it is being employed for the public good.

THE ADVERTISING INDUSTRY TODAY

Today, advertising is big business and getting bigger. The industry has shown phenomenal growth throughout the years and shows no sign of letting up. As communication technology improves, the opportunities for advertisers to sell their goods and services through various media increases. Advertising today includes newspaper and magazine space, television and radio time, direct mail, package design, special-market advertising, sales promotion, display and outdoor advertising, yellow

Table 1.1 Advertising Age 500 index—worldwide billings since 1983

Source: *Advertising Age*

pages, recruitment, and brand-new types of consumer advertising involving computer and cable technology. For those with the right combination of drive and creativity the advertising industry is definitely an environment in which such traits can be applied.

The advertising industry's growth is predicted to continue in the coming decades. According to the Bureau of Labor Statistics, advertising is expected to be one of the fastest-growing industries for wage and salary workers. Employment in advertising should increase at a rate of 2.9 percent a year through the year 2000.

The need for new people in the advertising field can be attributed to the fact that agency billings are increasing at a healthy rate every year. The more companies increase their advertising, the more people are needed to create and execute advertising campaigns. The *Advertising Age* 500 Index shows how billings for the top 500 agencies have increased over the last several years.

There are approximately eight thousand advertising agencies in the United States and an estimated 100,000 people work in these agencies, with two or three times that number working in corporate advertising departments and in other support areas of advertising. In most agencies, two or three people are employed for every $1 million in client billings.

Newcomers face tough competition for the limited number of openings each year. Despite continued growth, the popularity of the advertising business has always made it a difficult one to break into for newcomers. With perseverance, assertiveness, and a flair for creativity, one should be able to find a spot in this exciting field.

Corporate Advertising Departments

The American Association of Advertising Agencies estimates that there are only one thousand to twelve hundred agency openings each year for college or business school graduates. This figure does not reflect the total picture. An area of great opportunity in advertising that is often overlooked by college graduates is the corporate advertising department. Here, employees work for a corporation and become involved with every aspect of advertising while also participating in the total marketing effort of the corporation. Although most such corporate advertising departments use the services of an advertising agency, there are others that have an "in-house" advertising agency complete with all the job opportunities that an outside agency offers. Young people tend to gravitate to working for an advertising agency, but the corporate advertising department can be every bit as challenging and rewarding as the conventional advertising agency. In corporate work if you are responsible for a successful advertising campaign, you might one day move up and become president of the company. This is especially true in markets where advertising is a major factor in determining the success of the company— such as packaged goods, personal care products, fragrances, and travel. A business-minded graduate seeking a job in advertising would do well to consider opportunities for work at Kraft or Procter and Gamble, as well as at Young & Rubicam or Leo Burnett.

Areas of Opportunity

There are many areas within the advertising industry where beginners can get their start. The following listing of career opportunities in advertising corresponds to the areas covered in the chapters that follow in this book where the reader will find more useful information. Keep in mind that these opportunities exist in both agency and corporate environments.

Creative services. This is where the ads are created. The finished products from this area include print ads, radio and television commercials, direct mail, catalogs, and packaging. Among the positions available in creative services in both agency and corporate settings are copywriter, art director, creative director, graphic artist, illustrator, photographer, TV producer, and mechanical artist.

Media services. Media planners evaluate and recommend where ads should be placed in order to reach the optimum audience and attain the

Table 1.2 Top 10 U.S. agencies by gross income/1988

Rank	Agency	Worldwide gross income
1	Young & Rubicam	$758,000,000
2	Saatchi & Saatchi Advertising Worldwide	740,000,000
3	Backer Spielvogel Bates Worldwide	690,000,000
4	McCann-Erickson Worldwide	657,000,000
5	FCB-Publicis	653,000,000
6	Ogilvy & Mather Worldwide	635,000,000
7	BBDO Worldwide	586,000,000
8	J. Walter Thompson Co.	559,000,000
9	Lintas: Worldwide	538,000,000
10	Grey Advertising	433,000,000

Source: *Advertising Age*

best response. Media buyers purchase space for ads in newspapers and magazines and time for commercials on radio and television. Other positions in media services include media director, media supervisor, broadcast media supervisor, and media estimator.

Research. Agency and nonagency researchers attempt to identify the audience that the client wants to reach. Researchers also run tests on creative material to gauge its effectiveness in reaching and influencing the desired audience.

Account management. Account executives, in the agency setting, represent the agency to the client and the client to the agency. They are responsible for coordinating the advertising campaign and making sure that the agency and the client are satisfied with the advertising program. In the corporate setting, the equivalent of the account executives may well be the advertising managers or directors and have the same responsibilities except they do not answer to a client, but to the company they work for. Positions in this area include management supervisor, account supervisor, account executive, account coordinator, and account assistant.

Production and traffic. Print production turns the copy and artwork into finished advertising. Broadcast production handles the making of a television or radio commercial from casting to the final edit. The traffic department schedules and keeps track of all production and creative work and makes sure that all ads are finished on schedule and delivered on time.

Agency management and administration. These are the people who administer the agency or corporate advertising department. Positions in this area include president, chief executive officer (CEO), partner, chief financial officer, and accountant. The financial administrators oversee client fees and billings, talent payments, production costs, and all matters relating to salaries, expenses, and benefits while also making sure the agency prospers.

Media sales.   A career in media sales involves the sale of advertising in various media to advertisers and their agencies. Sales positions can be found in all types of media, magazines, newspapers, television, radio, and outdoor advertising firms. An often overlooked option for those seeking careers in advertising, media sales provides an excellent overview of the entire business due to the many contacts one makes as a media sales representative.

Other areas of opportunity include public relations, direct mail, sales promotion, and marketing.

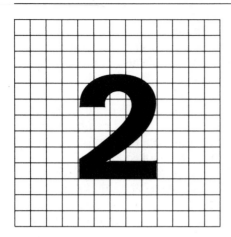

CAREERS IN CREATIVE SERVICES

The creative departments are the most visible and constitute probably the most challenging and demanding work in the advertising business. Success in creative work can be extremely rewarding. To see your own work in a magazine or on television and to know that your ideas contributed to the success of your client's product or service is a great source of personal satisfaction. Creative services attract young people. Agencies are always looking for fresh, new perceptions and ideas, and they often find these among young employees. Creative services is where ads are created and where the reputation and profitability of an advertising agency is often made or lost. While all of the agency functions are important and contribute in one way or another to the success of the advertising campaign, the end product—the advertising itself—is what the client is most interested in, since that is what the public sees or hears and either responds to or ignores.

The people in creative services are copywriters, artists, photographers, commercial producers, and creative directors. Any one of them can be the originator of a bright new campaign, a brilliant idea, or a new approach that convinces the public to buy the advertised product. People in creative services should be first-rate professionals in their specialty.

THE CREATIVE TEAM

In the creative department, teamwork is an important element in the development of a successful advertising campaign. At most agencies, a copywriter and an art director team up to create the ads for the client. When a TV commercial is required, the team may consist of a copywriter, an art director, and a producer all working under the direction of the creative director. The size and makeup of the creative department vary, of course, from agency to agency, and are influenced by the nature of the advertising the agency provides. Still, almost all ads created today are the result of collaboration by many talented people.

Ads were not always created by teams. Bill Bernbach, the legendary creative director of Doyle Dane Bernbach and leader of the creative revolution in the industry in the 1960s, is generally considered the one who first introduced the team concept. By pairing copywriters and art directors, he did away with the old system of having the copywriter first write the ad and then hand it to the art director for layout and design. The division of labor in the creative department is not always set in stone. Art directors may have ideas for copy and copywriters will frequently come up with great visual ideas. The creative process is give-and-take, the bouncing of ideas off of one another that most times will result in innovative and effective advertising.

Though the creative process may be a team effort, individuals still maintain separate identities and responsibilities and follow career paths unique to their specific work. An individual will apply for a specific job and will be teamed up later, usually by the director of the creative team. No two agencies have exactly the same structure, but most have in common such positions as copywriter, art director, producer, and creative director.

COPYWRITER

The copywriter has the responsibility to write the ads. He or she is responsible for the script for TV and radio commercials, for the headlines and text of print ads in newspapers and magazines, for the words that appear on billboards, and the product descriptions we see in catalogs and on the sides of cereal boxes and other consumer packaging—essentially all of the written words associated with advertising.

The copywriter is responsible for the "catch-phrases" that are often the basis for an entire advertising campaign. For example, "Don't leave home without it" for American Express and "Fly the friendly skies" for United Airlines are slogans that have been used successfully year after year. Often, a few words created by a copywriter can set a company's public image. When slogans are proved successful they are often used in TV and print ads for many years. Writing copy is not the same as writing articles, books, or poetry. Although all such writing is creative, advertising copy has a more definitive role in that it must sell a product or service. Furthermore, it has to be written to satisfy a client. Every ad must stand on its own, yet each ad must be fully integrated into a campaign that is consistent with the marketing objectives of the client. The copywriter must also be aware of competitive products and must write copy that positions the client's product favorably.

The copywriter's job does not end when the ad is written. In a television commercial, for example, copywriter, art director, and producer must decide on such elements as format, music, and effects. When the initial idea is complete, the copywriter may get approval from the creative director, who then will show it to the staff people who deal directly with the client. Changes may be required, and the copywriter must be flexible and willing to revise the work or have it revised by others. Copywriters in agencies are often required to participate in the presentation of the proposed ads to the client. The client may have suggestions for changes that, most likely, will have to be implemented. The final product often is unrecognizable when compared to the copywriter's original work.

Jobs in Copywriting

The entry-level position in copywriting is junior copywriter. Junior copywriters work on a variety of projects in order to learn the ropes. Since so many young people seek jobs in copywriting, starting salaries are low. Individuals can move up from junior copywriter to copywriter and then to senior copywriter, gradually gaining increased responsibilities and pay. As copywriters progress up the ladder, the work becomes more challenging and they have the opportunity to become involved in the conceptual side of creative advertising. The larger advertising agencies generally employ a copy director who oversees a staff of copywriters, decides who will get which assignment, and supervises the day-to-day activity of the copywriting staff.

What It Takes to Be a Copywriter

In order to be successful as a copywriter, a person must develop certain skills and personal attributes. Copy must be clear and persuasive and aimed directly at the audience for which the ad has been created. Depending upon the situation, the style may be formal, informal, or technical, but in all cases, it must succeed in getting across the central message of the advertising campaign. When promoting products and services, the best copywriters create ads that contain one simple idea expressed clearly, memorably, forcefully, and persuasively. When asked to communicate more complex ideas, copywriters must be clear, logical, and precise. A good copywriter must have the ability to express both simple and complex ideas in a manner that will bring about a response from the audience it is intended to reach.

It also helps if the copywriter has an appreciation and understanding of good design and illustration and how they work together and contribute to the effectiveness of a good ad. An understanding of all elements of an ad by everyone involved on the creative side helps the creative team to function as a more unified and versatile unit. Copywriters should recognize the fact that the illustration or the visual portion of a print ad or TV commercial are as important, if not more, than the copywriter's words. Furthermore, the copywriter may be required to tailor the text to fit the visual elements of the ad. It also helps if the copywriter has an understanding of the technical side of advertising production.

Copywriters must know what has succeeded in the past and must be able to take advantage of the proven techniques that are known to be successful. All creativity need not be new. It is equally important to be creative in knowing how to use or modify that which has proved successful.

Copywriters also need a thorough understanding of the legal issues affecting the claims that are made in promoting a particular product or service. Copywriters are not solely responsible for knowing all of the regulations, of course, but experienced writers will know how to avoid possible trouble.

Copywriters need to cultivate enthusiasm and curiosity about their client and the products to be advertised, and they need to immerse themselves in the client's marketplace in order to see what is going on. Being aware of trends and changing public attitudes gives copywriters a definite advantage in creating new and exciting advertising that will capture the attention of the public. They need to know as much as possible about their clients' competition, what consumers are buying, and what "the trade" (retailers, clerks, salespeople, distributors, wholesalers, and agents) are up to and their concerns. In short, the copywriter needs to have a clear understanding of the environment in which the advertising will appear.

Copywriters should also try to get to know their clients personally in order to become better acquainted with their ideas, their products, and their objectives. For the copywriter, being well informed is essential to success.

THE ART DIRECTOR

Like that of the copywriter, the job of art director requires talent, versatility, and the ability to adapt to many different tasks and situations. Besides being creative, the art director must be able to implement ideas and to channel creativity in a way that leads to the finished ad. An art director has to think as well as feel. Without organization and the ability to work with others, an art director might only come up with ideas that most likely would never see the printed page or TV screen.

The art director handles the visual side of the ad. Working in tandem with a copywriter, and perhaps a TV producer (if the message is for television), the art director provides the part of the ad that the public sees first. The chic model in an apparel ad and the action of a group of young people in a soft-drink commercial reflect the creative imagination of the art director. As mentioned before, teamwork is essential in the creative department, and an art director must be flexible and prepared to make changes when the team agrees that they are needed.

The art director's work falls into three stages: (1) conception, (2) presentation, and (3) production. First, a visual idea is conceived in the art director's mind; next it is discussed with others on the staff; and then, after modifications have been made, it goes on to the client. When the client approves the work, it goes into production. The art director is intimately involved with every step of this process and his or her input is vital through the completion of the ad.

Art directors have a demanding job that often requires late hours and working weekends to meet deadlines. In the case of TV commercials, art directors must frequently travel for on-location film production. For an airline starting new service to the Pacific, this might mean a week of production on a beach in Hawaii. Along with such occasional pleasantries, the job is filled with pressure.

Jobs in the Art Department

Traditionally, entry-level positions in the art department of an advertising agency or corporate advertising department include assistant art director and bullpen artist. Working in the art studio, or as it is commonly called, "the bullpen," is something that every aspiring art director must experience before moving up the art department ladder. In an advertising agency, the art studio is the last stop before the artwork goes to the client. All creative work that calls for design or illustration passes through the art studio. Here, layouts and photos are mounted, headlines are changed, mechanicals are prepared, or a TV storyboard is put together. One thing is for sure—working in the "bullpen" is never boring. This is where up-and-coming art directors learn their craft, master their skills, and work closely with more experienced art directors.

The higher up you move in the art department, the more conceptual and less hands-on your job becomes. The next position up from assistant art director is junior art director, which is also a job that entails a good amount of work on layout, paste-up, and mechanicals. The junior art director has more responsibilities and works more closely with the art director than the assistant art director.

The art director and senior art director are responsible for supervising the staff and creating and approving the ideas for the actual ads and seeing that these ideas are implemented by the rest of the art department. At this level in an advertising agency, one can expect more contact with the client and the client's advertising department and more interaction with other departments in the agency.

The top position in the art department is executive art director. This person runs the art department, oversees all employee and budget matters, and is often an active participant in client presentations. Though much of this position is administrative and supervisory, the executive art director works on the conceptual part of all of the more important advertising campaigns.

The salaries of art directors are basically the same as copywriters at similar levels. As with copywriters, the salary starts off low and increases quickly as one moves up the ladder. Advertising is an extremely popular field among artists. Department of Labor statistics show that more artists work in advertising than in any other field.

**What It Takes to Be an
Art Director**

Art directors have special skills and talents, just as writers do. Some are best at designing print ads, while others may excel at writing television commercials. Art directors who work on print ads must be adept at organizing elements of type and illustration so that they appear clear, uncluttered, and easy to read, and motivate the reader or viewer. The print ad must be effective in getting the advertising message across quickly and accurately. Art directors must have an extensive knowledge of typefaces and sizes and how they contribute and influence the readability of the ad. To illustrate how important this knowledge is, take a look through any magazine and see for yourself how some ads are much more appealing and readable than others. Successful ads are products of an art director who understands what works, both technically and conceptually.

Art directors also need to have a sense of what form of visuals will make the greatest contribution to the effectiveness of the finished advertisement. Should photography be used? Should the visual be a cartoon? Should it be a drawing? Should it be black-and-white or full color? Whatever it is, should it be bold or soft? The way in which an art director answers these questions can have a profound effect on the final product and its effectiveness.

Once the decision as to the art form has been reached, the next step is to decide which artist or photographer is best suited to produce the desired effect. Larger agencies sometimes have art buyers to handle this task; but in most cases, art directors perform this job themselves.

A background of training in art school or a school of design is a definite plus for those seeking this type of work. It is imperative that art directors be able to draw or sketch well enough to clearly demonstrate to the client how the finished ad will look, even though someone else may take care of the final artwork.

The design of a television commercial is also in the hands of the art director, but the producer generally controls the decisions relating to the visual makeup of a commercial. Again, a team is involved that must work together to insure that the highest-quality commercial is produced. Many of the same principles that apply to quality print ads apply to quality TV ads, and the art director must be adept at creating striking visuals, both on the printed page and on the screen.

THE PRODUCER

The TV producer is responsible for the creation and production of the television commercial. The producer must coordinate all parts of the project—the concepts, the people, and the technology. The producer does not usually contribute the specific ideas for the commercials, but contributes a great amount of influence over the final form of the commercial. The area of expertise that is uniquely the producer's is the technical area, including film and sound technology, which is extremely important in television production. Working with the art director and copywriter, the producer takes care of the many details involved in the casting and shooting of a TV commercial, and oftentimes contributes new ideas to the project as it evolves.

Usually, the copywriter and art director approach the producer with an idea in the form of a storyboard. By looking at the storyboard, the producer can determine the logistics of producing the idea and whether it is practical and effective. When it is decided that the project can be done, the producer hires a production crew, a director, and a casting director. The producer is also responsible for adhering to a budget and must make sure that the project is completed on schedule and that the client is happy with the final results. The job entails a great deal of contact with people and, as usual in the advertising business, long hours and unpredictable work schedules.

While art directors doing print ads have a limited range of design alternatives, producers have available all of the processes and devices of film and sound recording—animation, superimposition, close-ups, long shots, fade-ins, fade-outs, computer graphics, claymation, stop-motion, slow-motion, on-location filming, and a host of other optical tricks and special effects. The experienced producer is familiar with the entire range of techniques and knows which will enhance the persuasiveness of the ad's message while still adhering to the project's budget.

The production of TV commercials is an art form calling for great talent and imagination on the part of those involved, particularly the producer. The best commercial producers will have a preconceived idea of the desired effect before the shooting commences on a commercial. Experimentation can occur on the set. However, it must be limited by the budget, and it is the producer's responsibility to make sure things do not get out of hand financially.

Commercial producers also help decide on the jingle, sound effects, and background music that may be used in the commercial. And the producer works with the casting director to select actors, actresses, and, perhaps, animals for the production.

The importance of the casting director in the production of TV commercials cannot be overlooked. Casting directors screen applicants for parts in commercials and select those who appear best suited for the environment and message of the commercial. Casting directors generally keep files on available talent and know the talent agencies in town and the actors and actresses they offer. Casting directors must be proficient in the field of television to be able to evaluate the appearances, mannerisms, and voices of performers as they relate to the style and purpose for which the commercial is being produced.

Jobs in the Production Department

The entry-level position in the production department is production assistant. The production assistant, who works long hours for little money, helps the producer with all the details of the production. The junior producer, or associate producer, is given rudimentary production work, including test commercials and radio spots. The junior producer works more closely with the producer than the production assistant, and, of course, assumes more responsibility than the production assistant. With experience comes the promotion to producer and the opportunity to oversee the production of full-fledged TV commercials. The salary levels for producers fall slightly below those of copywriters and art directors at comparable levels.

THE CREATIVE DIRECTOR

The creative director in an advertising agency is the guiding force behind the creative output of the agency. He or she is an experienced advertising professional with the necessary talent and innovation to spearhead the entire creative staff. This position is arguably the most culturally influential of all jobs available in advertising. Sometimes the creative director is actually the head of the entire agency. It is a highly visible position that has been held by many "legends" in the advertising business, including the previously mentioned Doyle Dane Bernbach, famous for his innovative ads for Avis, Alka-Seltzer, and Volkswagen in the 1960s. Another well-known creative director is David Ogilvy of Ogilvy & Mather. He began his small agency in 1948 and turned it into one of the largest agencies in the world.

In the end, the creative director is responsible for the success of the advertising campaign. Creative directors are intimately involved with all aspects of the makeup of ads and must be knowledgeable about all of the areas in the creative department, including copywriting, design, and commercial production. The creative director must pull together the best team of writers, art directors, and producers and maintain a consistently high level of productivity and creativity. The creative director in many ways is a cheerleader in encouraging staffers in the department to boost creativity and productivity and must also cultivate new talent in order to keep the creative output fresh and current.

A creative director must also have a good head for business, as the position calls for participation in the running of the agency. Budgets must be watched and the day-to-day business needs of the agency must be administered in order to maximize the agency's profits. The creative director must also be acutely aware of client's needs and objectives, for often the client turns to the creative director for assurance and intelligent decision making during the development of an advertising campaign. As a result, the creative director must be articulate and capable of selling the agency's recommendations.

Most creative directors start out in the art department or as copywriters. It is in these positions that budding creative directors show their talent and ingenuity by creating successful ads and demonstrating leadership capabilities necessary for promotion to the higher agency ranks.

The climb up the ladder can be tedious or fast, depending on the progress would-be creative directors show early on in their career. Some rise to creative director in as little as five years; it is possible to reach this position before the age of thirty as the advertising business is quick to recognize young talent.

The rewards of being creative director are great—both personally and financially.

HOW AN AD IS CREATED

Understanding how an ad is put together from start to finish will help you understand how creative services works as a unit and will help to show the importance of the "team concept" that exists in most agencies.

Print Advertisements

Copy. While it is nearly impossible to separate the importance of the copy in a print advertisement from that of the artwork, good copy still remains the backbone of most successful ads. When first presented with the challenge of a new campaign, the copywriter must be sure to understand the objectives and strategy behind the advertising. This knowledge is essential if the copy is to sell the product effectively. Often the creative director will provide direction and guidance in this area. The copywriter will often work closely with the client's advertising department, in order to insure the client's satisfaction with the direction of the advertising campaign.

Next, the copywriter may develop several headlines, or leading statements for the ad, that convey the primary selling points of the product. This is the stage where the "catch-phrases" that we so often associate with a particular product come into being. In some instances, copywriters prefer to write the headline and then the copy; in other instances, the copy is written first and the headlines are derived from the body of the copy. The headlines, of course, are the most prominent and most visible part of the print ad. A good headline or catch-phrase will both convey the message of the product simply and clearly and grab the reader's attention. Many headlines are witty, based no doubt on the theory that if it is clever you are more likely to remember the message.

Design. While the copywriter is working on the written material, the art director is developing the visual part of the ad. However, the order of this procedure varies; sometimes the copy is based on an existing visual. Often the design is influenced by the direction of the headline, so the artist may not begin work until at least the headline of the ad has been developed. Once an idea has developed on how the ad should look based on the campaign strategy and preliminary copy, the art director develops one or more rough layouts showing where each of the elements of the ad are positioned in what will ultimately be the final version of the ad. The layout includes a rough drawing indicating what the photographs or illustrations will look like, where the copy and headline will be placed, and the location of any other components such as the logos, symbols, or disclaimers.

Mechanical.   Once the layout and the copy have been reviewed and approved within the agency, the copy and a more carefully prepared version of the ad, called a comprehensive or comp, are shown to the client. This process can involve a staged presentation or may be handled more informally, but one way or the other before any more work is done on the ad, the client's approval is necessary. Once the client approves the comp, the next step is the preparation of a mechanical.

A mechanical consists of all of the elements of the ad placed in exactly the position and size as they will appear in print. In order to produce a mechanical, the agency first typesets the copy in the type style and size indicated by the art director. This task is usually handled by an outside firm, or typesetting house. However, with new computerized typesetting, many agencies are setting at least some of their copy in-house. The next step is having the copy proofread for possible mistakes, which are noted by an in-house proofreader.

While this is taking place, the photo or illustration has been created and is placed on the layout of the mechanical. The actual processing of the photo on to a printed page is handled by the printer. If the illustration or other portions of the ad are to be done in color, the colors are indicated on sheets of tissue that overlay the ad. The actual print production of the ad will be discussed in a later chapter.

Broadcast Advertisements

Up to a point, processes involved in putting together a print ad and a TV or radio commercial are very similar. In both cases, the advertising strategy and plan are identical, but the ad itself and the medium in which the advertising appears are different. Instead of headlines and copy, the copywriter must develop a script for the ad. And rather than a layout, the art director, together with the producer, begins work on a black-and-white storyboard for the commercial. The storyboard resembles the boxes in a long comic strip.

Scripts.   A television commercial script is divided into two parallel portions. On the right side of the page, the copywriter indicates the sounds that will be heard in the commercial, including all spoken dialogue, music, and sound effects. On the left side of the script, the writer indicates what visuals appear on the screen during the time when each sound is heard. For example:

Visual	**Audio**
Dog eating dog food out of a bowl that bears the client's logo.	ANNOUNCER: Make your dog a happy dog. Feed him America's favorite dog food...

Many of the same rules for writing effective advertising print copy also apply to writing scripts for commercials. The opening statement should be brief and should attract the viewers' attention. Situations should be believable and simple enough so that the storyline of the commercial does not interfere with the ad's main goal—to sell the product! Furthermore, the scriptwriter/copywriter should remember that in a TV commercial the visuals carry more than half the weight of the ad in the audience's mind. The written material should support rather than dominate the commercial.

Design.   As with print ads, the design of a TV commercial is generally created after at least a preliminary script has been approved. At this stage, the art director and the copywriter prepare what is called the storyboard. A storyboard is exactly what it sounds like—a series of drawings mounted on a board, showing the action that takes place in the commercial. The number of frames in a storyboard varies from approximately eight to twenty, depending on the complexity of the commercial. The audio portion of the commercial plus any instructions on what the visual portion should look like are printed at the bottom of each frame. The storyboard serves as a guide to the actual shooting of the commercial. It is in this form that the client first gets an idea as to what the final commercial will look like and can make the decision as to whether to go ahead with the project.

Production.   Once the script and visuals have been approved by the client, production begins. Here we will discuss commercials that use live actors and actresses. Commercials using animation, special optical effects, and other production specialties are handled by various specialized professionals.

The first step in the production of a TV commercial is for the director of the commercial (either an employee of the agency or an outside expert hired to direct the spot) and the art director to begin casting the commercial. Actors and actresses who generally fit the descriptions of the characters in the commercial are auditioned and hired. Animals, if necessary, are screened and hired. Next, sets and outside locations are determined, and the necessary permits obtained. All props and wardrobe, including a large supply of the product to be advertised, are gathered together. The director and the agency then decide on the technical personnel that are needed for the production. Camera operators, lighting and sound technicians, makeup artists, hair stylists, and stagehands to move scenery and heavy equipment are among the people needed to produce even the simplest commercial.

On the day of shooting, light and camera crews may spend several hours setting up and lighting the set. During this time, the director may coach the actors and actresses on their lines and map out the action that will occur in the commercial. Long delays are common during the filming process, due to changes in lighting and rearranging the set between scenes. In the end, shooting a one-minute TV spot can take a whole day or more.

Postproduction. In the postproduction phase, the many pieces of film and sound created during the shooting are assembled to begin the process of forming the finished commercial. The film is edited into its proper order and the sound that has been recorded during the shooting is synchronized with the visual. Any recorded voices, music, or sound effects are added at this point. After a final review by the agency and the client, the film editor completes the final, or answer print, of the commercial. The film is then duplicated and sent to television stations, which will carry the commercial.

As you can see, creating an ad, no matter how brief and simple it may appear when you see it in a magazine or on TV, requires the efforts and cooperation of many people in creative services. These people must work as a team to produce quality work on schedule and within budget. Teamwork is the key to a successful advertising campaign.

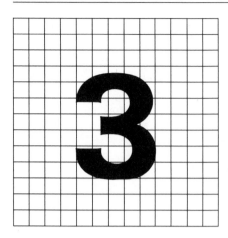

MOVING AHEAD IN ACCOUNT SERVICES

Account services plays an extremely important role in the success of every advertising agency. The people who service the agency's clients can be thought of as the center around which revolve all the other people in the agency. Account services help to coordinate the activity of all of the agency departments and are responsible for making sure that the client receives the best possible work and the best possible service. Perhaps more than anyone else, the account executive serves as the conduit between the client and the various departments of the agency, such as media, creative, research, and production. The account executive also makes sure that the account continues to grow in billings and profit.

The account executive must be personable, articulate, and have a good head for business. He or she must know sales and marketing and—most of all—must be able to sell the client on the creative work that is presented by the agency. Enthusiasm and knowledge of the client's products in the presentation of the agency's work are important characteristics that are found in successful account executives. An account executive must motivate and encourage the agency people involved in the work for the client and must be able to resolve in a calm and controlled manner any conflicts and differences that arise. Good people skills are essential for anyone hoping to become a successful account executive.

Along with the client and the client's advertising department, the account executive formulates the approach of the advertising campaign, identifies any marketing weaknesses, and looks for the best strategy to increase the client's sales in the future. The account executive works closely with the people at both the agency and the client's marketing and sales departments in order to pinpoint the marketplace for particular products and to determine the demographics and the psychographics of the type of consumers that are expected to buy the products. Together with the media department of the agency, the account executive makes certain that the client's money is spent effectively and efficiently. Account services also works in tandem with the creative department to ensure that the client's wishes are taken into account in the development of the creative elements of the campaign. Account services is the department that interacts the most with the other departments of the agency.

THE FUNCTIONS OF AN ACCOUNT EXECUTIVE

The functions of an account executive are demanding and diverse. It's fair to say that no two days are alike. To excel in account work, an individual must combine sound business judgment, a high level of proficiency in advertising, and the ability to interface well with people. An account executive's responsibilities fall into five main categories: (1) planning, (2) coordination, (3) presentation, (4) regulatory matters, and (5) agency profit management.

Planning

The account executive must plan the advertising with the client and others within the agency. Together, they decide the goal of the advertising—that is, the ideas that are to be communicated. They define the audience that is to be reached and the appropriate media to be used, the amount of money required, and the standards for measuring the advertising campaign's effectiveness. The planning stage is where the foundation and execution of the advertising campaign are determined.

To establish a sound advertising plan, the account executive must become knowledgeable in the client's business. He or she must know the sales and profit goals of the client, as well as what the client's competitors are doing and if they are succeeding and why. All of these factors are important in the planning stage.

Since account executives must deal more and more with economic, statistical, and financial concerns, an increasing number of advertising account executives are MBAs. Previously, account executives were known for their social skills and salesmanship. But as advertising has become more of a science, more and more account executives have found it advantageous to have advanced business degrees.

Coordination

Since an agency's work is the product of the efforts of many different specialists and departments, it falls on the account executive to make sure that all of the elements of the agency's output are brought together on time and consistent with the objectives of the campaign. The account executive must oversee the work of creative people, media specialists, producers, researchers, production and traffic, and often, outside suppliers. All of which means that the account executive needs to have a thorough working knowledge of each area of the business. The account executive essentially serves as liaison between the agency staff and the client.

The account executive must be a good judge of copy and must be sure that the advertising presented to the client is precisely on track and does not stray from the client's objectives. The account executive must possess an understanding of art and layout, in order to judge material to be presented to the client. In short, a good account executive must be an imaginative and a sound critic whom colleagues respect. He or she must be tactful in the evaluation of the work of co-workers and must persuade these same people that suggested changes are needed and justified. A person in this position tries to avoid compromise while still making everyone happy, while concentrating on coordinating an effective advertising campaign.

The account executive must recognize the strengths and weaknesses of the different forms of media and be able to translate this knowledge to the assignment at hand. This means having the reasons why magazines or television, say, are best for a client's needs. This is not to say that account services handles the functions of media services, but people in account services need to have the knowledge of the work of all agency departments.

The account executive must be up-to-date on production requirements for broadcast and print media and the costs and time factors involved in all areas of production. He or she must be familiar with the variety of research sources and techniques and must understand their applications, using good judgment about what research can and cannot uncover and when it might be used effectively. If the campaign calls for point-of-sale displays or special packaging, the account executive must be well informed about sources and what will work best.

Finally, and most importantly, the account executive must know and understand the people within the agency—the members of the agency team—and must have a sensitivity for the pressures connected with their jobs and the ability to motivate and stimulate them to do their very best work. In this light, the account executive is like a football coach, leading and inspiring a team of professionals to reach a defined goal.

Presentation

The account executive is usually responsible for presenting the agency's recommendations to the client. In this capacity, the job consists of two parts. First, when an advertising campaign is underway, the account executive will have frequent, often informal, meetings with the client to discuss details relevant to the campaign, and to present new commercials or written copy for approval. The matters discussed in these meetings may include the extension of media commitments, analysis of the budget, and changes in copy and in layouts. Second, when the time comes to present a new plan or campaign, especially one that departs from the course that has been followed, the presentation becomes more formal. In such instances, the agency usually makes the presentation to explain to the client the reasoning behind the new ideas and proposals and to show samples of new headlines, layouts, storyboards, and concepts. In these meetings, there are apt to be a number of client people present who are not normally involved in the day-to-day advertising decisions.

At these meetings, it is the account person's responsibility to organize and stage the presentations. Is it to be a formal presentation with slides and flip charts, or is it to be a low-key discussion around a conference table? Is the proposed advertising to be in its final finished form, or will it be presented by rough layouts or storyboards? How many agency people will actively participate in the presentation, who will they be, and what role will they play? Will the creative director or art director join the meeting? What about the copywriter? This aspect of the account executive's job is a little like being a theatrical director and producer. A winning presentation is often determined by the thoroughness and excitement of the presentation and the effectiveness of the presenters.

Regulatory Matters

As mentioned in an earlier chapter, there exists a growing body of governmental regulations that control the content of advertising. The account executive must be familiar with this ever-expanding body of rules. He or she also should be familiar with the codes and practices of publishers, stations, and networks in order to be in a position to negotiate on matters affecting the client's interests and the success of the advertising campaign. A good knowledge in this area can help avoid a variety of possible regulatory problems that could interfere with the efforts of the agency and the client.

Agency Profit Management

In addition to the other duties and responsibilities, the account executive, must also be responsible for the profitability of each account. Agency management will always be ready with reminders that the agency must attain its profit objectives. Every account is supposed to contribute to profit. Accordingly, the responsible account person must monitor the people power and time that each account absorbs. Profit management is simply another one of the many hats that the account executive must wear.

Other Responsibilities

Beyond the work that involves the development of new strategies and new campaigns, the account executive takes care of maintaining the day-to-day business of the account. Account executives spend time getting to know the client and collecting new information and insights into what makes that client tick. It is extremely important for the account executive to have a good feel for what is going on at the client's company.

The account executive is also responsible for scheduling, making sure that ads are completed, accurate, and placed at the proper time. Though other agency departments handle much of this work, account services is ultimately responsible if an ad is late or incorrect.

Account people also deal with a lot of paperwork in their jobs. This generally includes "contact reports," which are summaries of the communications between the account executive and the client. These contact reports can include records of telephone calls, correspondence, and accounts of meetings and presentations. Writing reports and summarizing meetings is time consuming, but this information is essential to keep track of points that were agreed on or comments made by the client at all stages of the campaign. With the dozens of changes that an ad can go through during production, it is crucial to know who said what, when, and to whom.

An effective account person can balance the necessity of concentrating on the details while keeping in mind the overall strategy and goal of the advertising. Too much emphasis on memos and meetings can stifle the creative side, and too little attention to the details can make for a confused and ineffective campaign.

Account executives find that writing is a significant part of their work. This writing can include presentations, internal memos, letters to the client, and reports on meetings with the client. A great deal of information passes from the agency to the client and from the client to the agency, and all of this generally passes through the account person. The account person who is a good writer becomes an effective communicator of this important information. Unlike copywriting, this writing is not creative but must sell the agency's ideas to the client and represent the client's position to the agency. A clear, concise, persuasive writing style that also incorporates the technical and intuitive sides of advertising is desirable.

Account people with out-of-town clients can expect to do a lot of traveling. Often, when TV commercials are involved, the account executive may be away from home for as much as a month at a time. For some, this is a chore, and for others, it is viewed as an exciting part of the job.

JOB OPPORTUNITIES IN ACCOUNT SERVICES

According to the Bureau of Labor Statistics, a good percentage of the available jobs in the area of marketing, advertising, and public relations managers, are found in the field of advertising. These management jobs include those positions available in account services.

The future of the job market in account services looks quite promising at this time. The U.S. Department of Labor expects at least a 30-percent increase in the number of jobs in this field by the year 2000.

Assistant Account Executive

This position is considered as the entry-level position in the account services department. It is a good place to view the inner workings of the department and to learn from the more experienced account executives. The assistant account executive's responsibilities usually involve a lot of paperwork and legwork. The job calls for administration, execution, analysis, compiling statistics, conducting studies, keeping records, and monitoring a myriad of details. It also entails the need to attend meetings and seminars and, basically, to observe the work of agency staffers.

In some agencies, though, an assistant account executive may start early in working as the key agency contact on smaller accounts or on one particular brand or product within a large account. For example, an assistant account executive might be given full responsibility at a breakfast cereal account for a new variation of an old brand or a new size cereal package that will have its own campaign. The assistant account executive also must learn what people in other agency departments do and how this work relates to the client. All of this information must be assimilated quickly in order for the assistant account executive to function effectively. Often, just when the assistant account executive is comfortable with an account, he or she is switched to a different account. Frustrating as this may seem, such moves are often required to serve the changing needs of clients and will give the fledgling account executive a broader base of knowledge and skills for the future.

Usually an assistant account executive will report to one account executive. At some agencies, the assistant is put through a company training program preparatory to beginning work on specific accounts. Each agency tends to have its own program for the training and advancement of employees in account work. It often takes a few years to be promoted to account executive.

Account Executive

The next step up the ladder in account services in the position of account executive. As expected, this job is less administrative and more conceptual than the job of assistant account executive. More of the job is devoted to working directly with the client and the client's advertising department on ways to increase the client's sales, than is devoted to the day-to-day business of the account department. Like the assistant account executive, the account executive gains knowledge and experience through working with the client and other departments in the agency, but the account executive's involvement is deeper and the responsibility greater.

The account executive is generally the key person on any given account and carries the responsibility to maintain contact with the client to the degree that is necessary to ensure that the client's needs and wishes are serviced properly. The account executive's day usually includes meetings with agency people in such departments as creative or media and phone conversations or meetings with the client. As we mentioned earlier, detailed records must be kept of all contacts and the account executive is responsible for overseeing this record keeping.

Usually, the account executive deals with tasks and problems as they occur during the course of the day. It is a job with constant changes and a great deal of unpredictability.

Account Supervisor

The position of account supervisor is the next step up from account executive. The difference is in the fact that the account supervisor usually handles two to four different products or clients.

The account supervisor spends less time than the account executive worrying about details and more time in supervision, and is most likely to have on staff two to three account executives. Therefore, the account supervisor must be familiar with the work of these staffers and have the ability to delegate and oversee such work.

In this supervisory capacity, the account supervisor becomes increasingly aware of the big picture within the agency. Lessons learned on one account can be applied to another. The account supervisor has a greater influence on the overall success of the agency.

Of course, the more experienced an account executive becomes, the less supervision is needed. At that point, the account supervisor can devote more energy to troubleshooting and conceptual account strategy. Like the account executive, the account supervisor maintains a close relationship with the client's advertising department and often is involved with the highest level of corporate management.

Management Supervisor

Continuing the climb up the account services ladder, we next encounter the position of management supervisor. The person in this position usually has control of two to three account supervisors. Often a management supervisor will oversee several major products from a large client or several different clients. The management supervisor is less involved in the day-to-day business of the client and more involved in planning campaign strategy and helping the client make sound marketing decisions.

Management supervisors work closely with high-level management and the director of the client's advertising department. They also are responsible for keeping an eye on the profitability of each account and how these accounts benefit the agency. The management supervisor will study account budgets, review major creative work and major marketing reports, and make sure that the agency staff is functioning efficiently.

Account Director

A number of the larger agencies have a position that ranks above management supervisor—account director. The account director may be in charge of one or two big accounts, including all products and brands, and will have two to three management supervisors on staff. The person in this position is heavily involved in managing the agency and developing new business, as well as overseeing the business of account services. In rare circumstances, an agency will have a position above account director—that of group account director. The group account director supervises the account directors in the agency. Again, the employee structure of an agency depends largely on the agency's size and the number of accounts it handles.

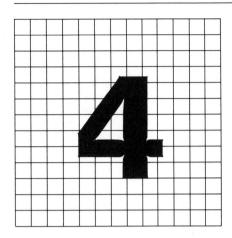

OPPORTUNITIES IN MEDIA SERVICES

In order for advertising to sell a product or service effectively, it must be read, seen, or heard, and acted upon by the right audience. It makes no difference how good the advertising is; if it does not reach the proper people, it is relatively worthless. This is where media services comes in. This agency department has the responsibility of evaluating, selecting, and recommending the publications, stations, and programs that will expose the advertising to the widest possible effective audience. And since clients pay to advertise in these media, media selection and media buying commands great attention in the client-agency relationship.

The media services department in advertising agencies has grown in importance in recent years. Before television and radio there were not many media specialists. But today, with such a wide selection available and coupled with the high cost of space in print media and the high cost of time on television and radio, media buying and media selection has become a science and has taken on greater importance.

Consider, if you will, the powerful presence of network television, the appearance of specialized cable networks, satellite broadcasting, and the increasing number of magazines and newspapers, and you can readily understand that media specialists are important and are in great demand. As such, opportunities in media continue to grow. These people are playing a more major role in the strategic planning of advertising campaigns and the operation of advertising agencies.

Media services performs three major functions—evaluation, selection, and buying. Let's take a closer look at these three areas and how they interface within the operation of media services.

MAJOR FUNCTIONS OF MEDIA SERVICES

Media Evaluation   People involved in this work are generally referred to as media planners. They are responsible for developing the media plan, which is the outcome of the process of media evaluation and selection. This process begins with media research. Every agency of any size has a research library, and large agencies subscribe to a great many different research services. These services supply huge amounts of data on reading, viewing, and listening habits, as well as profiles of the readers and viewers attracted to various publications, TV and radio programs, and even such things as outdoor billboards. In addition, planners need basic information on the media, such as advertising rates, deadlines, and mechanical specifications.

The primary sourcebook for basic information for newspapers, magazines, radio, and television stations is *Standard Rate and Data Service,* commonly referred to as SRDS. Separate editions of SRDS are published to provide information on newspapers, consumer magazines, business magazines, radio, and television. The information covers circulation and viewer information, costs of different units of space or time, frequency discounts, and coverage of each station or publication. For many years this was considered the only reliable source of information about the media, but there were some facts SRDS did not report, like the ages, incomes, life-styles, and buying habits of media audiences. Services, like Nielsen, Arbitron, MRI, and Simmons, now provide this type of more sophisticated information. The Nielsen and Arbitron rating systems provide a wealth of statistical information about TV and radio audiences that is extremely valuable to the media planner. Simmons Market Research Bureau (SMRB) and Mediamark Research Inc. (MRI) both measure the demographics of magazine readers. They also supply supplemental data on newspapers, radio, and television, and information on product usage and consumption. They select a national, projectable sample of twenty thousand adults and compile demographic, marketing, and media information. Other services attempt to measure psychographics. This covers people's life-styles and interests, likes and dislikes, attitudes and beliefs, prejudices, and patterns of use of one product over another. The media planner must make use of these resource tools in order to conduct a successful media evaluation and provide a solid media plan.

By using these resource tools, a media department can give a car manufacturer, like General Motors or Nissan, some assurance that its new-car advertising is aimed at the right type of buyer. Until quite recently, it was very hard to have any degree of assurance about such distinctions, but computerized data banks have greatly increased our ability to store and sort many pieces of information.

In today's agency, the computer is making a substantial contribution to media research and selection. Let us consider an advertiser with a large budget and an advertising plan specifying the use of magazines and network TV to reach women between the ages of twenty-four and thirty-five. The aim is to reach the greatest number of these women the greatest number of times. The media planner puts together a list of magazines and programs that are good possibilities and submits the list to the assistant planners. The assistant planners then feed the information into the computer, and the computer reports back the best combination of media that will get the desired result with the greatest efficiency.

There are also extensive files of other more commonplace data in the agency's media research library. This information includes material obtained from the sales representatives from print media and radio and television stations describing the characteristics of their audiences.

Media planners are more than just keepers of these records. They must be able to evaluate this material and decide what is reliable and relevant. This skill requires that they understand the techniques used to collect their data and whether such procedures are valid. They make the final decisions about which research services the agency will buy or subscribe to and the extent to which these services will be used. Their jobs require analytical minds that find statistical investigation both fascinating and challenging.

Media Selection

Media selection is the job of putting together a recommended schedule utilizing the available information. This is done in the most precise way possible and by combining media that will be read, heard, or viewed by those people most apt to respond to the advertiser's product or service. This task begins with an understanding of the advertising plan—the audiences to be reached, the requirement for repetition, the length of the advertising message, and the money available to carry out the task. This understanding is fundamental to making intelligent choices. Media selection is initially the responsibility of the media planner; it is subsequently reviewed by others in the agency.

Network TV is far and away the most popular medium for advertisers of general consumer products, obviously due to the huge numbers of people that can be reached through this medium. Table 4.1 lists the national ad spending by media for the 100 leading national advertisers in 1988. Here, we see how media have been selected.

The first step in media selection is to single out one or more categories of media that are best suited to fulfill the objectives of the advertising campaign. From that point on, the planner, with the assistance of the research team, selects the markets, stations, programs, and time and days of the week for radio and TV ads, and the publication and dates of insertions, size of ads, and often, positions for magazine and newspapers. Everything is tailored to a precise schedule. Equally important is the job of juggling dollars and insertion dates until they fall into place in a fine-tuned schedule. Due to knowledge and creativity and a good understand-

Table 4.1 Total national ad spending by media

Category	100 Leading National Advertisers Ad spending			% total	
	1988	1987	% chg	1988	1987
Magazine	$2,597.1	$2,360.4	10.0	8.1	7.8
Newspaper supplement	186.4	138.5	34.6	0.6	0.5
Newspaper	2,351.9	2,155.3	9.1	7.3	7.1
Outdoor	274.8	257.0	6.9	0.9	0.9
Network TV	6,985.7	6,499.8	7.5	21.7	21.5
Spot TV	3,452.0	3,479.6	(0.8)	10.7	11.5
Syndicated TV	685.6	570.6	20.2	2.1	1.9
Cable TV	402.1	331.2	21.4	1.2	1.1
Network radio	420.5	391.7	7.4	1.3	1.3
Spot radio	592.7	531.3	11.6	1.8	1.8
Farm publications	32.0	32.3	(1.1)	0.1	0.1
Subtotal measured	17,980.8	16,747.7	7.4	55.8	55.5
Estimated unmeasured	14,227.6	13,446.2	5.8	44.2	44.5
Total ad spending	32,208.5	30,193.9	6.7	100.0	100.0

Note: Dollars are in millions. Source: Leading National Advertisers Multimedia Service, as compiled and published by Leading National Advertisers.

ing of available media, the process of media selection has become a real science.

One of the fastest-growing areas in media is cable television. In recent years the media planner has seen cable take on a more influential role. As cable reaches more and more people, its importance to advertisers will become even greater. Table 4.2 lists the top cable networks by estimated gross advertising billing for 1988 and 1989. These are the cable networks that attract the most advertising.

Table 4.2 Top cable networks by gross advertising billings ($000,000)

Network	1989	1988	% change
1. Turner Broadcasting System	$244.1	$230.5	5.9%
2. ESPN	173.5	147.0	18.0
3. Cable News Network	164.5	143.0	15.0
4. USA Network	137.0	109.6	25.0
5. MTV: Music Television	93.0	80.0	16.3
6. Lifetime	85.3	68.2	25.1
7. The Nashville Network	83.5	72.5	15.2
8. CBN	68.6	55.3	24.1
9. Nickelodeon	42.0	35.0	20.0
10. Turner Network Television	27.2	0.6	4,433.3

Note: All figures estimated: TBS estimates do not include Atlanta market billings, estimated at $21 million in 1989; CNN figure includes Headline News billings.

Source: Paul Kagan Associates. Reprinted from *Advertising Age.*

Table 4.3 1988's top magazines in ad revenue

'88 Dollar Rank	'87 Dollar Rank	'88 Revenue (000)	% Change, '88 vs. '87
1. Time	2	$349,742	+6.4
2. TV Guide	1	335,408	+1.3
3. Sports Illustrated	4	323,872	+23.1
4. People Weekly	3	305,342	+14.7
5. Newsweek	5	241,714	+1.0
6. Business Week	6	227,320	+4.5
7. Better Homes & Gardens	7	152,806	+7.5
8. Fortune	11	137,406	+12.6
9. Family Circle	10	134,358	+8.4
10. Good Housekeeping	8	129,288	-2.4
11. Forbes	9	128,748	+0.2
12. U.S. News & World Report	15	128,141	+20.8
13. Woman's Day	12	115,650	+0.2
14. Cosmopolitan	13	114,574	+2.7
15. Reader's Digest	14	113,971	+6.3
16. Vogue	17	87,493	+10.0
17. Glamour	16	87,023	-0.7
18. Ladies' Home Journal	19	83,772	+9.2
19. Money	18	79,767	+1.5
20. Redbook	21	68,558	+5.7
21. McCall's	20	62,592	-7.6
22. Rolling Stone	23	62,073	+12.5
23. Southern Living	22	61,652	+5.9
24. Elle	34	55,417	+42.1
25. Golf Digest	27	55,274	+22.3

Source: PIB/LNA Magazine Services, as compiled and published by Leading National Advertisers.

If the media plan calls for radio advertising, selection of powerful general audience stations may be important if the advertised product is for the mass public. On the other hand, if the product is male-oriented, advertising on a radio station broadcasting the local baseball game may be the best choice. If you want to reach teenagers, you might choose stations featuring pop music.

When selecting magazines, the media planner must be acutely aware of the demographics of audience and the readership. One would not place an ad in *Field and Stream* to reach women. This may be obvious, but it takes extensive research to determine which magazine is best for a particular product or service. Advertising in magazines has a longer life, and with so many titles to choose from, the media planner can generally find special-interest magazines that pinpoint ideal readers for the advertised product. With the increase in the number of new magazines and the increase in magazine ad revenue, magazines are playing a larger role in the schedules of many national advertisers. Tables 4.3 and 4.4 list the top magazines by ad revenue and the top ten types of products that are advertised in magazines, with automotive ads leading the way.

Table 4.4 Magazine ad revenues for PIB's top ten classifications

'88 Rank	'87 Rank	Ad Class	'88 Revenue (000)	Change vs. '87
1	1	Automotive	$800,587	+17%
2	3	Toiletries & Cosmetics	553,909	+22%
3	4	Direct Response	466,946	+9%
4	2	Business & Consumer Services	465,902	-6%
5	5	Food & Food Products	376,866	0%
6	7	Apparel, Footwear & Accessories	362,543	+11%
7	6	Cigarettes & Tobacco	351,866	+5%
8	8	Travel & Hotels	311,308	+12%
9	9	Computers, Office Equip. & Stationery	251,639	+4%
10	10	Beer, Wine & Liquor	212,988	+2%
		TOP 10 TOTAL	$4,154,554	+8.4%
		ALL OTHER CLASSIFICATIONS	$1,788,195	+9.2%
		TOTAL ALL CLASSIFICATIONS	$5,942,749	+8.7%

Source: PIB/LNA Magazine Services, as compiled and published by Leading National Advertisers.

The tables displayed in this chapter are examples of the types of information that will influence media planners in their media selection. In addition to using this data and other data available in the research library of the agency, planners involved in media selection continually meet with the sales representatives of specific media to learn more of competitive situations and changes within the media. In order to stay up to date, they must spend considerable time meeting with these media salespeople and assessing the validity of their data and comments.

Good media planners must be analytical and comfortable with figures, imaginative and well informed, interested in the broadcasting and publishing businesses, and alert to the importance of the intangible (or unmeasurable) aspects of each medium. As in every other advertising job, planners must also be eager to find innovative ways to do their work.

Media Buying

Media buying is the next step. Buying advertising space in a magazine or newspaper is relatively easy since most publications have unlimited space for sale. It is, however, not so easy in the case of radio and television time, particularly television spots on top shows. For example, there is a limited number of spots to be sold on the telecast of the Super Bowl, and you can be sure that advertisers of automobiles, beer, and other products with appeal to men will scramble to be first in line. Often, preference is given to those advertisers who purchase time throughout the year and to those advertising agencies that are big TV spenders. Generally, media buyers are given the specifications, such as dates, markets, and audience demographics, against which they must find the best spots for the advertiser's purposes. They then determine from the sales representatives what spots are available—known in the trade as "avails." With this information in hand, buyers will negotiate for the purchase of the avails that best meet specifications and budgets. Since the rates quoted by most broadcasting stations are quite flexible, purchasing is truly a matter of negotiating, and professional and knowledgeable buyers can stretch the clients' budgets substantially by skillful negotiation. Obviously, the stations and networks stand firm on rates for top shows and prime time slots, but for spots on the late, late rerun at 2 A.M. of a 1960 flick from Hollywood, there is considerable flexibility in rates. Frequently, buying is done on the basis of oral commitments that are later confirmed in writing. For this reason, it is absolutely essential that both buyers and sellers live up to their agreements scrupulously.

The best buyers are good at detail, effective data analysts, and work well under pressure. When things get busy at the agency, buyers are very busy. It is work that calls for a special skill in negotiation and persistence. A buyer who does well is often moved up to a position in media supervision, or more senior management jobs, although some people choose to make a career of media buying and can do very well financially.

Within advertising agencies, media personnel spend a tremendous amount of time with sales reps from the media. Such representatives are either employed full time by the media (such as the major networks, which have their own staffs); or, in the area of broadcast, they may be employed by an independent representative organization, such as John Blair, which represents independent radio and television stations. A firm like Pattis/3M specializes in the representation of magazines and has advertising sales personnel operating out of offices throughout North America and Europe. These sales people receive training in the demographics and buying characteristics of the readers of the magazines they represent so that they can assist the advertising agency's media personnel in assembling and evaluating the data required for their media recommendations.

The most active media buying occurs in the area of broadcast. The peak season for network TV media buying is in early May when the networks announce their fall TV schedules, and the buying activity lasts through the end of July or August. Buyers must be knowledgeable about the new and returning shows and their content and appeal. Unlike print buying, where the rates for advertising space are fairly well set, broadcast buying is a constant game of wheeling and dealing. The variability of rates is greater and the money spent can be enormous. Broadcast buying is more demanding than print buying, though print buying calls for its own special kind of expertise. In buying space in magazines and newspapers, there can be rate flexibility for the big advertiser, but most negotiating centers around preferred positioning of the advertisements in the magazine, special treatment in merchandising, and in the case of less successful publications, editorial support for the advertiser.

MEDIA SERVICES AND ITS RELATIONSHIP TO OTHER AGENCY DEPARTMENTS

Media services personnel must be able to work well with other departments in the agency and with the clients. Input from the client's advertising department is invaluable to the success of a media plan and should be actively encouraged by the media department. Interaction with other agency departments occurs on a daily basis and can be of great benefit to the media department. The following paragraphs describe how media services works together with other agency departments to help execute an advertising campaign.

Creative services.   Media people interact with creative people to take advantage of new opportunities that media people learn from media representatives. Often media people learn first about what has worked for others and what did not. Media services are on the lookout for new developments within the media and attempt to measure the impact these developments might have on the media plans for the clients of the agency. Media people often advise the creative staff about alternative and often ignored media, such as billboards, transit-car cards, and perhaps even skywriting and advertising on park benches.

Research.   Media services use the research department to provide analyses of demographics and other statistics that influence media buying. The research department is an important source to media people concerning population shifts and geographic characteristics. It also provides competitive information on client activity.

Account services.   As we mentioned in the last chapter, account services performs the role of being the representative of the client to the agency and vice versa. It is vital that media services personnel interact well with those in account services, as these people are responsible for coordinating the overall advertising plan and for making the client's wishes known to other agency departments.

JOB OPPORTUNITIES IN MEDIA SERVICES

Assistant Planner

The typical entry-level position in media planning is that of assistant planner. In this job a person gathers statistics for media planners and becomes acquainted with the basic research tools discussed earlier in this chapter. An assistant planner can expect to spend considerable time working with facts and figures and will gradually begin to understand the meaning behind this information and how it influences the media plan. This research and statistical work provides the media planner with the materials to develop a full-fledged media plan.

Junior Buyer

On the media-buying side, the entry-level position is known as junior buyer. Like the assistant planner, the junior buyer is mostly involved in working with numbers, lots of paperwork, scheduling, and placement. It is a position where one learns the basics of media buying. It is the first step to becoming a media buyer. This training period is necessary and usually does not last more than a year or so.

Junior buyers make about the same as assistant planners.

Media Planner

As we mentioned before, the media planner is responsible for media evaluation, media selection, and development of the media plan. He or she will work with the information gathered by the assistant planner and then suggest a definite plan for the client. Usually, a media planner will have had at least two years experience in the media department before being elevated to this position.

Media Buyer

Media buyers take care of buying space in print and broadcast media. Besides negotiating media buys, these people track budgets and schedules and provide post-analysis reports. Junior buyers usually graduate to the position of media buyer a bit faster than assistant planners graduate to the position of media planner.

Media Supervisor

Normally, a media supervisor will have worked as an assistant planner and as a media planner before being stepped up to this position. A good knowledge of those positions is a requisite for this job. This position involves a great deal of overseeing and providing guidance to planners and assistant planners and a lot of contact with the heads of other agency departments and the client's advertising department.

Broadcast Supervisor

The broadcast supervisor coordinates the buying operations of the media department. In this position a person serves as supervisor to the buyers and junior buyers and usually negotiates the larger and more difficult buys. The broadcast supervisor insures that the department work is completed as scheduled. A person in this position must be intimately aware of everything that is taking place in the broadcast industry as well as current trends and all the happenings in broadcast programming.

Associate Media Director

This position calls for more involvement with the administration of the agency and the agency's long-term projects and goals. The associate media director works with planners and buyers as well as with the client and other agency departments, especially account services. Often this person carries the title of vice-president.

Media Director

The media director is the head of the entire media services department. This person has the responsibility to be sure that all planning and buying moves along smoothly for the benefit of the agency and client. The media director makes sure that the staff is of the highest professional standing and working to the best of their abilities. A person in this position can expect to hold the title of senior or executive vice-president in the agency and to play an important role in shaping agency policy and the direction of future growth. Generally, the media director is heavily involved in the presentations for new account solicitations and will often be included in important meetings with top clients of the agency.

RESEARCH: IDENTIFYING THE BUYERS

Many think of researchers as numbers crunchers who are only concerned with statistics, printouts, reports, charts, and graphs. Others perceive researchers as those people who stifle creativity by highlighting the cold reality of numbers into the planning and development of the advertising campaign.

While it is true that these factors play an important role in advertising planning, it is also true that the human element plays an equally important role in the work of a good researcher. Advertising research is about people—their likes and dislikes, their attitudes and beliefs, their lifestyles and buying habits, and perceptions of the marketplace. Researchers try to find out not only *what* people are buying but *why* they buy. It all comes down to understanding people and human behavior and what makes them tick. Data is important, but what it tells us about the people behind the data is more important. In a nutshell, the research department can be thought of as the representative of the consumer within the advertising agency.

Today, the trend in agency research departments is away from statistics and demographics and toward cultivating a better understanding of the consumer. The researcher may use one-on-one interviews, psychological profiles, analyses of attitudes and behaviors, as well as psychographics (the psychology or motivation behind consumer actions) to get to the heart of the question, "What is our consumer like?" The warm, comfortable, person-to-person ads that appear on TV these days can be looked at as a product of this new approach in advertising research. By better understanding the people who purchase the client's product or service, the research department can better help the client to reach out to more consumers and increase sales. Researchers develop strategies based on their findings that help the agency and client work toward the goal of increasing sales. We can say then that the primary responsibility of the researcher is to identify the buying consumer for the client.

The research department works closely with the creative department and with the client's advertising and marketing departments. Though many times researchers fall into particular specialties, such as consumer studies, media research, market research, and copy testing, more often than not today's research department contains generalists—those who can handle all areas of research and consequently focus on the needs of a single account. This way, the researcher becomes extremely knowledgeable about a specific account and is thus better able to respond to problems and offer solutions.

RESEARCH SOURCES

The research department looks to two basic areas for data: original and secondary sources. Original research is that which is conducted by the research department itself. The direction of this research is decided by the client and the research department and can include interviews in shopping malls, telephone surveys, mailed questionnaires, computer analyses, and the hiring of outside research firms. Secondary research can be defined as any outside data that helps to define consumer trends and behavior. Secondary sources include magazines, newspapers, independent studies, books on consumer attitudes, corporate studies, or anything that the agency or client did not specifically commission. Often the client has its own research department that works in tandem with the agency's research department.

VALS and Consumer Behavior

One of the new ways of looking at consumer behavior is by means of the VALS categories, a psychographic method. VALS, which means Values and Life-styles, is a system of placing the consumer into psychological types. This system was created by SRI (formerly known as the Stanford Research Institute). VALS are divided up into four categories:

1. Need drivens—Those with limited financial resources who are driven more by need than choice.
2. Outer-directeds—Those whose buying habits, attitudes, and activities are influenced and shaped by what they think others will think.
3. Inner-directeds—Those who live their lives according to inner values rather than the values of others.
4. Integrateds—Those whose inner-direction and outer-direction are combined into a functional entity.

Researchers work to determine where the target audience falls for a particular product or service in the VALS spectrum. This knowledge can be extremely helpful to the planning of an advertising campaign.

Market Simulation Testing

Another valuable research method is market simulation testing. This is where a group of people are shown advertising for a particular product and then are taken to a mock store, given "money," and asked to shop. Researchers can determine how effective the advertising is by how many of the respondents "buy" the product. Many times this procedure is repeated a few weeks later to determine whether the "consumer" will purchase the product again. This test is useful in helping the agency and the client decide if the product is worthy of introduction into the marketplace.

Market Research

Market research is more often undertaken by the advertiser, but it is frequently carried out by the agency research department or by a specialized research firm.

Market research, the basis of modern marketing decisions, involves determining what areas of opportunity are open to a manufacturer and the kinds of packaging, pricing, distribution, and promotion that will make the manufacturer's product successful. The following is a list of the major information sources utilized by market researchers:

- Government statistics, an incredible source and readily available and free to everyone.
- Trade, business, and industrial magazines that serve specific fields.
- Business statistics assembled by various trade associations and business groups.
- Client information, which is the private and, often, closely guarded property of the advertiser.
- Syndicated services that provide information on the movement of an advertiser's goods and those of competitors on the retail market. Without these services, it is very hard to tell what is happening to products after they leave the factory. This is particularly true in the case of packaged goods such as cosmetics, prepared foods, and drugstore items.
- Visits to the "trade," which involve going into the marketplace to find out what dealers, retailers, and salespeople are doing to help or to hinder the sale of an advertiser's product. This kind of investigation is of particular value when a number of competitive products are sold in the same stores. Salespeople can have a strong influence on sales of products based on their own preferences.

Table 5.1 Top 10 U.S. research organizations

Rank			Research revenues	
1988	**1987**	**Organization**	**1988 total**	**'88–'87 % chg**
1	1	A.C. Nielsen*	$880.0	20.5
2	3	IMS International*	365.0	22.0
3	2	Arbitron/SAMI/Burke	320.0	(1.5)
4	4	Information Resources	129.2	22.5
5	5	Research International	103.4	9.1
6	7	MRB Group	78.2	28.0
7	6	WESTAT	64.3	5.3
8	8	M/A/R/C Inc.	51.1	1.6
9	9	NFO Research	40.9	5.1
10	10	Maritz Marketing Research	39.9	4.7

Notes: Dollars are in millions. * indicates that company revenues are *Ad Age* estimates. Source: *Advertising Age*.

- Specially commissioned private research that gives readings on the attitudes and behavior of various consumer groups. This type of study is valuable when the manufacturer is not too clear about consumer attitudes but knows that they are important to successful marketing. Table 5.1 lists the top independent research firms in the United States—the firms that agencies turn to for research assistance and special studies during the development of an advertising campaign.

WHAT YOU NEED TO MAKE IT IN RESEARCH

Those who expect to succeed in the field of research need to be analytic and have a natural curiosity about people. You should feel comfortable with numbers and be able to interpret data, but extensive training in mathematics and statistics is not necessary. Attempting to understand the many variables of human behavior is the best training you can hope to have. This type of knowledge is gained through life experience and is invaluable to the researcher.

An ability to search for and find pertinent information is requisite for a job in a research department; you will be using many sources in your work, and it will be necessary to sift through a great deal of information in order to get to the information you need for your current project. Researchers must be enthusiastic followers of trends and developments in consumer attitudes, opinions, habits, and life-styles. They should also be clear and persuasive communicators, both orally and in writing.

People in research must continually ask themselves how they can use their findings to help increase the sales of the client's product or service. Researchers may find themselves working closely with the client's marketing department in order to find new ways to increase a product's visibility and market penetration. By combining their efforts, these two departments can offer strong support to any advertising campaign.

JOB OPPORTUNITIES IN RESEARCH

Research departments are generally smaller than the other agency departments, and many agencies send a good deal of their work to independent research companies. Many of the positions listed below would only be found in larger ad agencies, and these positions generally will vary greatly from agency to agency.

Project Director

There are two levels of project directors in the research department—junior project director and senior project director. The position of junior project director is considered to be the entry-level position. Project directors focus their energies on gathering facts and background information without analyzing the information. Being able to organize the data in a way that senior researchers can understand and interpret is the mark of a good project director. Project directors may be involved in the writing of questionnaires, the coordinating of surveys, and the conducting of one-to-one interviews.

Research Supervisor

This position, sometimes referred to as research account executive, is the next level up from project director. The person in this position begins to assume supervisory responsibilities. Along with coordinating the more complicated research studies and writing research proposals, the research supervisor keeps an eye on the project directors and assigns their work. The research supervisor is more involved with specific research studies for the client and therefore has more contact with the client than the project directors.

Associate Research Director

The next step up the research ladder is the position of associate research director. People in this position are expected to have at least ten years of experience in research. These people work most closely with the client and other agency departments, especially creative services and account services. Associate research directors supervise the activities of outside research firms hired by the agency and the activities of their own research staff.

Research Director

After about fifteen years in research, one may be promoted to the position of research director. A person in this position is usually a specialist in a particular area of research. The research director is responsible for assigning work to staff members and maintaining a productive working environment. As the head of the research group, this person represents the department to the client and has more say in the agency's direction as a whole.

Executive Research Director

Some of the largest agencies also have the position of executive research director—the absolute top of the heap. This person has research directors on staff and usually is involved in the management of the agency. Much of this position is supervisory.

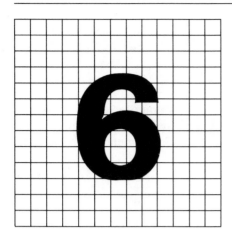

JOBS IN PRINT PRODUCTION AND TRAFFIC

In some advertising agencies, print production and traffic are combined into a single department; in others, they are separate. Regardless of the arrangement, these departments work so closely together that it is often difficult to determine exactly where one leaves off and the other begins. Needless to say, print production and traffic are extremely important to running a smooth and efficient advertising agency. Please note that broadcast production, which is closely related to print production, is covered in the Creative Services chapter of this book.

TRAFFIC

This department can be likened to the air traffic control tower at an airport. It is the department where timetables and deadlines that govern an agency's activities are monitored. Traffic is responsible for seeing that all of the elements of an advertisement or commercial are fitted together and forwarded to the designated medium in the proper form and on time. The material can range from type and illustrative elements needed for engravings or photoreproduction for print advertisements to audio transcriptions for radio commercials.

Traffic is a matter of coordinating, obtaining approvals at each stage of the ad's development, meeting deadlines, and seeing that everything goes smoothly and according to plan. Traffic people help others in the agency to do what they should when they should. Directing the flow of work in and out of the agency and between various agency departments is the heart of the traffic department's responsibilities. Like account services, traffic falls in the middle of the action at the agency and thus is usually considered a stepping-stone to a position in account services.

Deadlines are probably the most crucial part of a job in traffic. Each publication has its own deadline for ad placement. Missing a deadline can seriously hamper an agency's advertising plan, especially if the ad must run at a certain time (for example, in a Friday newspaper for a weekend sale). Fortunately, good traffic people are extremely thorough and conscientious and rarely miss deadlines. Often, people in the department will keep an eye on each other and watch out for the mistakes that contribute to missing a deadline.

Directing Traffic: What It Takes

Good traffic planners need, above all, to be orderly and well organized. They need to be able to manage a great amount of detail accurately. They must know all about the processes that are involved in the creation of an advertisement, with special understanding of the amount of time needed to complete each step. They must also be able to track and move along a number of projects at one time. Patience and quick thinking come in handy when directing an advertising agency's traffic.

Traffic people must also be able to deal effectively with outside suppliers and with members of the creative team at the agency. They must know which creative people respond to coaxing and which ones need to be shaken up in order to get them to meet deadlines. Meeting deadlines sometimes depends on the traffic person's ability to push others to complete work on time. A certain amount of finesse is essential in this job.

Traffic work can be demanding, but for those who enjoy it and do it well, it provides the satisfaction of knowing that you are part of the indispensable lubrication for the agency's gears.

PRINT PRODUCTION

Print production is responsible for buying the various elements that go into the printed material produced by the agency, including advertisements, pamphlets, brochures, outdoor posters, flyers, sales manuals, and direct mail material. The print production people deal with a large number of outside suppliers that offer a range of services and materials. These include typographers, engravers, electrotypers, photoreproducers, photostaters, printers, and free-lance artists. As a result, production people need to have source files of all the available facilities for each of these services and must know the strengths and weaknesses of each supplier. Having a good rapport with suppliers can be beneficial when deadlines are tight; suppliers may make special accommodations for those production people they know well. Basically, print production is responsible for insuring that a print ad appears in a newspaper or magazine as planned and on time. Print production works together with the art director to see that the art department's ideas are properly reflected in the final ad. The production person brings to the artwork the technical expertise that the art director may not possess. This collaboration between production and art director often results in a successfully executed and effective print ad.

A print production person must be knowledgeable about the engraving process, which affects not only how the artwork will ultimately look but how much it will cost to produce. There are three main engraving processes in use today—offset, rotogravure, and halftone gravure (which is a kind of combination of offset and rotogravure). The production supervisor will usually ask for bids from a few engravers, choose the best one, and then see the job through completion. Print production people must always keep up on the latest production trends and technical advances. A strong general knowledge of print production techniques is essential for a person working within this department.

Typesetting

Typesetting is also taken care of within print production. Some of the bigger agencies have typography managers and a typography staff. Like the production supervisor, the typography manager works with the art director but deals with type size and style. Once the art director and typography manager decide on type size and style, the typography manager will contact a typehouse to handle the actual typesetting for the ad.

Budget Control

Another area of responsibility for print production is budget control. Those working in print production need to know whom to contact not only to get a job done on time but also at a good competitive low price. In most cases, it is necessary to get competitive bids, particularly on large or complicated assignments and, of course, it is required on all government contracts. This requirement usually means added time and almost always requires extra paperwork.

Like those in traffic, good print production people need to be well organized and capable of giving close attention to the details of a number of projects that must be processed simultaneously. The production person must also know the amount of time each supplier needs to complete a job under normal circumstances, as well as the absolute minimum time each needs under the most urgent pressure.

Both traffic and print production can be career jobs for those who find this sort of work satisfying and rewarding. For the most part, however, they are learning jobs that serve as training for better paying positions in an agency, usually in account services.

As an important aside, in past years, almost everybody in an advertising agency started in one of these jobs. This is no longer true, but it is essential that account people, writers, and designers really understand the chemistry of print production and traffic activities so that they can cooperate and contribute to the smooth operation of the agency.

Art Buying

The buying of art is closely related to print production. In most agencies, art buying is a section within the print production and traffic department. In some agencies, it may be a separate department.

Buying artwork for advertisements demands knowledge, good taste, and negotiating ability, as well as the ability to understand the needs and objectives of creative people, especially the art director, for whose output the art is being purchased.

There are many parallels here to the job of a casting director involved in broadcast production. The art buyer must have extensive information about the talents of a varied number of commercial artists—from photographers, to illustrators, to cartoonists. Buyers must also know who is best qualified for fashion and who is best for photographs of, say, heavy machinery. All of which amounts to keeping a roster, not only of specialties, but of subspecialties as well.

Art buyers are also constrained by deadlines, and therefore must know who among the various artists or photographers is available to deliver on time and who is too busy to meet a required deadline. Buyers are also governed by budget considerations and must be able to deliver the quality of work required at prices that are acceptable to the client. In carrying out these tasks, good business judgment and a keen negotiating skill are musts. Art buyers must be sufficiently well organized to keep their records in order to make the job run smoothly and professionally.

Art buying is a fascinating and gratifying occupation for anyone who has a true appreciation of the whole spectrum of commercial art, who enjoys dealing with interesting and talented people, and who gets satisfaction from discovering new talent, and who enjoys helping aspiring young artists.

JOB OPPORTUNITIES IN PRINT PRODUCTION AND TRAFFIC

Traffic Assistant

This is considered the entry-level position in traffic. A person in this position reports to the traffic coordinator and is responsible for handling departmental paperwork, looking after details, and keeping an eye on deadlines. A college degree is not required for this position.

Traffic Coordinator

The traffic coordinator is the person who takes care of the actual shepherding of an ad as it makes its way to print. A person in this job can expect to have constant contact with the creative and account services departments. Some traffic coordinators also work closely with the client and the client's advertising department.

Traffic Manager

The traffic manager oversees the entire traffic department, including scheduling, supervising staff, and controlling the agency's print ad activity. Traffic managers see to it that their staff members are working well together and responding to the needs of the agency. Budgets and personnel matters are also the responsibility of the traffic manager.

Production Assistant

This position is the equivalent of traffic assistant, but on the production side. Production assistant is the entry-level job in print production and includes many of the basic duties found in this department. The production assistant reports to the production supervisor and handles a good deal of the paperwork. Again, a college degree is not necessary to break into this department.

Production Supervisor

This position is print production's equivalent to traffic coordinator. The production supervisor, sometimes called the buyer, is the person who actually deals with the suppliers and negotiates prices. The art buyer and typography manager fall under this job heading—they are simply different kinds of production supervisors.

Production Manager

The person in this position is considered the head of print production. The production manager assigns work to the staff and insures that all the work being done is up to professional standards. The production manager works closely with the heads of other agency departments and with the client to insure that the best print work is being done in the most cost efficient manner possible.

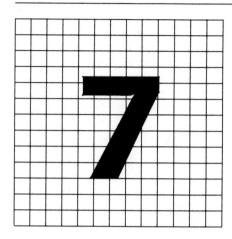

AGENCY MANAGEMENT AND ADMINISTRATION

In any agency, someone has to be in charge and someone has to attend to the administration of the agency's business. This chapter discusses the important role of agency chief executives and the functions of the agency administrative departments—financial management, legal services, personnel, office management, and various other support groups. As we will see, there are many interesting and challenging positions within the structure of an advertising agency's business side.

AGENCY CHIEF EXECUTIVES

The air is thin at the top. Only a few talented, hardworking men and women reach the pinnacle of agency chief executive. Natural leadership ability is a requisite for these positions and these people have risen to the top because they demonstrated their leadership talents all the way up the ladder. Though the job of chief executive can be extremely demanding, the financial rewards are great—many chief executives make over $500,000 a year, along with equity participation, options, and other perks.

No one department of an agency has a monopoly over another when it comes to producing chief executives. A look at the chief executives of many of the top agencies today will show that these people came from varied departmental backgrounds—from creative services, from account services, from media, and from research. Leadership is something that is found in many different areas of the advertising business, and those with natural leadership ability will rise to the top regardless of where they began their careers.

Agency chief executives are in charge of making sure that the agency's organization, finances, and output are achieving excellence in all aspects. Filling key management positions, assisting the client in building business, and taking care of long-range planning are all the responsibility of the chief executive. At the largest agencies, the chief executive is often responsible for overseeing worldwide operations. Traveling also plays a large role in the life of the chief executive, especially in an agency with many branch offices. It is a position that requires a great deal of physical energy and stamina.

A chief executive must also be good with people and know how to get the best work from the agency's management staff. Being good with people is also needed in dealing with clients. The chief executive is expected to be in personal contact with important clients, and the clients generally look to the chief executive for reassurance and counsel on improving their business and getting the most from their advertising.

It may seem that all of these responsibilities are too much for one person, so you find that in many cases there is more than one person at the top. Many of the larger agencies have an executive team that runs the agency and an executive committee that provides direction on important decisions. For example, the executive team may include a chief operating officer (COO), a chief executive officer (CEO), an executive creative director, and a chief financial officer (CFO). Generally, there is an agency president, and frequently there is a president for international operations. A liberal use of important-sounding titles also helps in client contact, as it enables the agency to parade high-level executives around the world to meet with clients and prospective clients.

The executive committee may also include senior people from each of the agency's departments. These committees act as a sounding board for the executive officers and will meet regularly to discuss problems, opportunities, and agency objectives.

At a small agency, you generally find one or two people at the top who are usually the owners or major partners. In such instances, one or two people are responsible for the major management decisions at the agency. Regardless of the arrangement, agency chief executives are the people who call the shots and influence the success or failure of the agency.

FINANCIAL MANAGEMENT

The main function of the finance department is to see that money comes in on time and bills and other obligations are paid on schedule. An agency's cash flow, and ultimately its profit, is what keeps it in business, and therefore the finances must be well managed.

Every agency places an enormous amount of space and time with the media each month. This places a great demand on the cash flow at the agency. Generally, clients are billed at the time space and time is ordered. As a result, the agency should receive payment from the client before the bill is received from the media.

If there is a breakdown in this arrangement (for example, a slow-paying client), the agency can find itself in a cash crunch. Therefore, managing cash flow at an agency is important. The finance department also manages the agency payroll and often supervises company benefits programs such as medical insurance, profit sharing programs, and retirement plans.

At many of the larger agencies, the finance department is divided into two principal areas—media billing and production billing. Those who work in media billing invoice clients for the cost of ad space and TV or radio time and pay the media promptly. In production billing, expenses for each production job are recorded as soon as they are determined, and generally after the work is completed, the people in production billing prepare invoices for review by the account people. There are many elements of expense in a production bill, and those who are involved with this work must be able to track the details and to organize the billing well. In some agencies, you will find media billers working in media services and production billers working in production and traffic, rather than being grouped separately in the finance department.

Most agencies have at least one person who is responsible for monitoring cash positions and for ensuring prompt collection of bills and prompt payment of supplier invoices. The larger agencies have both a treasurer and a controller to assume these responsibilities. They, in turn, are backed by clerical, secretarial, and supervisory personnel with qualifications the same as those for similar jobs in any other business.

Agency Compensation

Since we have been discussing the agency's financial management matters, it is probably a good time to address the subject of agency compensation.

Today, most agencies are paid a fee for their work. This fee may be paid on an assignment-by-assignment basis—the cost of the work of completing each ad or series of ads is billed separately.

In other cases, agencies work on a defined contract. The client and the agency agree that the agency will perform specific tasks over a given period at a specified cost. The cost of each individual ad and the production charges are billed to the client, but the cost is not to exceed the amount agreed upon in the contract. Agencies sometimes are asked to bid on a project, such as a new catalog, and will then contract to complete the project for no more than the stated sum. Agencies also are compensated in part by charging an add-on charge, for material or services bought from outside suppliers—artists, photographers, printers, film producers, and other such independent operators. The usual add-on for these outside purchases is 17.65 percent of the supplier's charges, which translates to 15 percent of the total amount billed to the client. This amount generally compensates the agency for the cost and profit for performing such services. Furthermore, fees are often charged for projects such as publicity and speech writing, sales promotion work, staging and conducting sales meetings, and any other service that the agency may perform.

In most cases, the agency also retains the 15 percent commission when paying media for space and time placements. The exceptions include retail ads in newspapers and other "noncommissionable" media. If a full page in a magazine costs $1000, the publication bills the agency $850. The agency bills the client the $1000, the amount the client would have to pay if dealing with the media directly, and retains the $150 commission. The amount retained by the agency provides income to the agency and may be the only income the agency receives from the client. In other cases, the client will pay the agency an additional fee or, in the case of a large user of commissionable space or broadcast time, the client may insist on a rebate of a portion of the commission or require that the agency perform certain services in return for keeping the large commissions. As the advertising business has become more competitive, it is now quite common for large advertisers to negotiate media commissions with their agency. For example, a large client may allow their agency to retain only 12 percent and expect rebates or other services to make up the difference between the 15 percent commission the agency receives from the media.

Keeping track of agency compensation and its complications and exceptions is the responsibility of the finance department.

LEGAL SERVICES

Since laws and regulations affecting the advertising business are in a state of constant development and refinement, most large agencies have one or more lawyers on staff to serve as advisers to the account services and creative services personnel.

These lawyers must review the advertising that the agency produces and make sure that it complies with the laws, rules, regulations, and customs that govern the advertising industry consumer protection laws. They usually review the first draft of ideas through the finished product. Lawyers also handle contracts for outside suppliers and performers that are hired for commercials, litigation, real estate and leasing matters, and essentially any legal matter in which an agency may be involved.

Agencies that specialize in serving clients in highly regulated industries, such as pharmaceuticals or securities, are more likely to have larger legal staffs. Agency attorneys also serve as a link to whatever outside legal counsel an agency may employ.

Advertising agency law is highly specialized and, although there are few job opportunities in the field, it can be fascinating and challenging because of the formative nature of the rules that govern the advertising business.

PERSONNEL

Personnel, often referred to as human resources, is another department in an advertising agency. People in personnel handle the business of employment—posting positions, conducting interviews, administering résumé files, and administering employee records.

Besides handling applicants for employment, personnel often manages the employee health and dental plans, benefit packages, vacations, and pensions. Personnel can also be involved in staff training programs and in helping to maintain and boost employee morale.

OFFICE MANAGEMENT

As in any business, personnel management is essential to the smooth operation of the agency. This work involves all of the housekeeping duties of the business, and in smaller agencies, may include the handling of legal matters.

BASIC SUPPORT

Like other businesses, agencies need secretaries, typists, clerks, receptionists, librarians, and information specialists. If the agency has a computer system, it may well need programmers, analysts, and machine operators similar to what is required at any other computer installation.

While the tasks involved in advertising support positions are similar to support positions in other businesses, the atmosphere is likely to be more lively and challenging.

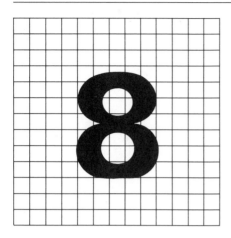

CORPORATE ADVERTISING DEPARTMENTS AND BRAND MANAGEMENT

Throughout this book there have been allusions to jobs on the corporate side. Now it's time to take a closer look at these career opportunities. As you will see, working in a corporation is by no means the same as working in an advertising agency. There are two distinct areas where people can build a career in advertising within corporations—the advertising department and in product management which is generally in the marketing or sales department. Both areas will be discussed a little later in this chapter. First, let's take a look at some of the basic differences between working at a corporation as opposed to an advertising agency.

THE CORPORATE SIDE VS. THE AGENCY SIDE

What you will hear most often about the differences between an agency and the corporate side is that the agency side is loose and casual, and the corporate side is conservative and structured. One could also say that the corporate side is...well...more corporate. This reality is something that should be kept in mind when deciding where you want to work. In the final analysis, your own personality and your long-term ambitions should determine where you are most likely to be comfortable.

The corporate environment also tends to be more rigid and mapped-out in terms of job levels and advancement. Corporate job descriptions are often detailed and very specific. Usually, corporate work tends to be more heavily administrative. Fiscal reports, budgets, market surveys, and evaluations play a big part in the day-to-day activity of the corporate advertising person. That's simply the way it is. It is also true that the higher you move up the corporate ladder, the further you are likely to move away from advertising.

If you want a lifetime of involvement in advertising, the corporate side may not be for you. On the other hand, you will certainly see more and learn more about all aspects of business by working within a corporation. Your career goals will influence your choice.

There are, however, attractive incentives for working on the client side—high pay and more control. Jobs on the corporate side tend to pay about 20 percent more than comparable jobs on the agency side, and this can be an attractive lure for someone considering working on the corporate side.

Perhaps the most significant difference is found in the fact that when you are on the client side, you are in control. The agency works for you. The agency carries the burden to please the client. As one agency old-timer said to a group of his young account people, "Remember the Golden Rule—he who has the gold makes the rules."

Agencies live in constant fear of losing clients. A morning's mail can carry enough terminations from clients to wipe out an agency—and all of the jobs that go with it. Therefore one must recognize that there is much greater stability and job security on the client side.

Working on the corporate side eliminates the frustration of always having to worry about client approval of your ideas and plans. Decision-making power is ultimately in the client's hands, and the client controls the direction and thrust of the advertising. If you enjoy the power of directing the advertising and don't mind the extra burden of the administrative work, a career on the corporate side may be for you.

Look at it this way: if advertising is your first love, work in an agency; if you are a businessperson at heart with an interest in advertising and marketing, build your career on the corporate side. Keep in mind that people can move back and forth between the agency side and the client side, so it is possible to try both areas and see which one suits you best.

The tables on the following pages will give you an idea of where the corporate jobs among the companies that do the most advertising can be found. Taken from *Advertising Age,* these tables list first ad spending in 1988 by the top 50 spenders and then the top ten advertisers in each media category—network TV, spot TV, spot radio, newspapers, and magazines.

CORPORATE ADVERTISING DEPARTMENTS

Corporate advertising departments offer attractive opportunities for lifetime careers in advertising. These departments set advertising policy for their companies, establish advertising goals, make sure the advertising prepared by their agencies is consistent with the company's sales and marketing objectives, and keep these agencies up-to-date on product development, research, market conditions, and top management's current thinking and concerns. The corporate department is the conduit between the agency and every department of the client company.

Table 8.1 Ad spending in 1988 by 50 leaders

Rank '88	Rank '87	Company/headquarters	Total spending	'88–'87 % chg
1	1	Philip Morris Cos., New York	$2,058,223	7.2
2	2	Procter & Gamble Co., Cincinnati	1,506,891	2.8
3	3	General Motors Corp., Detroit	1,294,000	34.0
4	4	Sears, Roebuck & Co., Chicago	1,045,185	4.4
5	5	RJR Nabisco, New York	814,537	(3.4)
6	40	Grand Metropolitan PLC, London	773,914	(2.0)
7	7	Eastman Kodak Co., Rochester, N.Y.	735,945	8.5
8	8	McDonalds Corp., Oak Brook, Ill.	728,320	10.7
9	6	PepsiCo Inc., Purchase, N.Y.	712,347	1.4
10	17	Kellogg Co., Battle Creek, Mich.	683,089	21.8
11	10	Anheuser-Busch Cos., St. Louis	634,531	4.4
12	11	K mart Corp., Troy, Mich.	632,000	0.0
13	15	Warner-Lambert Co., Morris Plains, N.J.	609,156	3.3
14	12	Unilever NV, London/Rotterdam	607,469	(4.0)
15	28	Nestle SA, Vevey, Switzerland	573,820	12.4
16	9	Ford Motor Co., Dearborn, Mich.	569,783	3.0
17	16	American Telephone & Telegraph Co., New York	547,504	3.1
18	14	Chrysler Corp., Highland Park, Mich.	474,009	0.1
19	13	General Mills, Minneapolis	470,058	3.0
20	20	Johnson & Johnson, New Brunswick, N.J.	468,835	5.8
21	26	Bristol-Myers Squibb, New York	430,693	1.6
22	18	J.C. Penney Co., Dallas	426,580	(5.5)
23	27	Quaker Oats Co., Chicago	423,420	12.6
24	21	Ralston Purina Co., St. Louis	420,973	(8.5)
25	NA	Time Warner, New York	409,715	17.1
26	120	May Department Stores Co., St. Louis	399,687	(4.5)
27	23	American Home Products Corp., New York	393,221	(0.3)
28	25	Coca-Cola Co., Atlanta	385,085	15.2
29	38	H.J. Heinz Co., Pittsburgh	340,089	22.1
30	24	Mars Inc., McLean, Va.	339,657	(14.0)
31	31	Sara Lee Corp., Chicago	326,944	19.6
32	NA	Macy Acquiring Corp., New York	308,879	2.8
33	30	Colgate-Palmolive Co., New York	306,624	4.9
34	36	Walt Disney Co., Burbank, Calif.	300,581	26.6
35	69	Hershey Foods Corp., Hershey, Pa.	298,631	17.5
36	29	U.S. Government, Washington	295,100	(5.2)
37	32	General Electric Co., Fairfield, Conn.	276,611	3.3
38	33	Toyota Motor Corp., Toyota City, Japan	272,945	18.3
39	NA	SmithKline Beecham, London	264,199	19.9
40	35	Schering-Plough Corp., Madison, N.J.	262,173	(0.6)
41	104	Campeau Corp., Toronto	260,467	(8.3)
42	34	American Cyanamid Co., Wayne, N.J.	256,165	(0.9)
43	131	American Stores Co., Salt Lake City, Utah	250,518	3.6
44	44	American Express Co., New York	247,201	5.9
45	37	Honda Motor Co., Tokyo	243,258	11.1
46	42	Tandy Corp., Fort Worth, Texas	232,026	0.4
47	113	Dayton Hudson Corp., Minneapolis	230,196	1.1
48	46	Pfizer Inc., New York	230,052	17.8
49	47	Nissan Motor Co., Tokyo	224,947	40.7
50	39	IBM Corp., Armonk, N.Y.	214,381	(3.5)

Note: Dollars are in thousands. Source: *Advertising Age.*

Table 8.2 Top 10 network TV advertisers

Rank	Advertiser	Network TV expenditures			as % of co.'s
		1988	1987	% chg	'88 ad total
1	General Motors Corp.	$443,402	$272,953	62.4	34.3
2	Philip Morris Cos.	388,602	376,628	3.2	18.9
3	Procter & Gamble Co.	370,175	377,552	(2.0)	24.6
4	Kellogg Co.	297,740	237,985	25.1	43.6
5	McDonalds Corp.	245,389	216,067	13.6	33.7
6	Anheuser-Busch Cos.	207,278	186,948	10.9	32.7
7	Unilever NV	189,652	213,481	(11.2)	31.2
8	Ford Motor Co.	175,688	161,177	9.0	30.8
9	RJR Nabisco	174,002	209,777	(17.1)	21.4
10	American Telephone & Telegraph	173,912	146,418	18.8	31.8

Note: Dollars are in thousands. Source: Leading National Advertisers Multimedia Service, as compiled and published by Leading National Advertisers.

Table 8.3 Top 10 spot TV advertisers

Rank	Advertiser	Spot TV expenditures			as % of co.'s
		1988	1987	% chg	'88 ad total
1	Pepsico Inc.	$257,957	$271,069	(4.8)	36.2
2	Procter & Gamble Co.	222,883	238,049	(6.4)	14.8
3	Philip Morris Cos.	157,578	176,159	(10.5)	7.7
4	General Mills	145,945	135,805	7.5	31.0
5	Grand Metropolitan PLC	130,339	142,005	(8.2)	16.8
6	McDonald's Corp.	128,102	129,010	(0.7)	17.6
7	General Motors Corp.	115,286	103,522	11.4	8.9
8	Anheuser-Busch Cos.	87,486	83,750	4.5	13.8
9	Hasbro Inc.	78,681	72,148	9.1	47.8
10	Time Warner	78,368	79,345	(1.2)	19.1

Note: Dollars are in thousands. Source: Leading National Advertisers Multimedia Service, as compiled and published by Leading National Advertisers.

Table 8.4 Top 10 spot radio advertisers

Rank	Advertiser	Spot radio expenditures			as % of co.'s
		1988	1987	% chg	'88 ad total
1	Anheuser-Busch Cos.	$42,696	$43,550	(2.0)	6.7
2	General Motors Corp.	40,185	34,829	15.4	3.1
3	Philip Morris Cos.	40,092	29,489	36.0	1.9
4	Pepsico Inc.	28,198	19,766	42.7	4.0
5	Sears, Roebuck & Co.	25,431	21,211	19.9	2.4
6	Southland Corp.	22,108	18,317	20.7	30.5
7	Grand Metropolitan PLC	21,090	16,366	28.9	2.7
8	Delta Air Lines	19,948	19,671	1.4	17.7
9	Chrysler Corp.	19,412	17,345	11.9	4.1
10	Procter & Gamble Co.	15,777	7,906	99.6	1.0

Note: Dollars are in thousands. Source: Radio Expenditure Reports.

Table 8.5 Top 10 newspaper advertisers

Rank	Advertiser	Newspaper expenditures 1988	1987	% chg	as % of co's '88 ad total
1	May Department Stores Co.	$224,282	$230,174	(2.6)	56.1
2	Macy Acquiring Corp.	182,212	176,033	3.5	59.0
3	Sears, Roebuck & Co.	160,969	175,052	(8.0)	15.4
4	Campeau Corp.	124,488	134,833	(7.7)	47.8
5	Dayton-Hudson Corp.	90,630	81,062	11.8	39.4
6	General Motors Corp.	86,835	83,841	3.6	6.7
7	Texas Air Corp.	82,441	66,647	23.7	64.0
8	Philip Morris Cos.	76,711	46,048	66.6	3.7
9	Carter Hawley Hale Stores	75,554	52,353	44.3	47.3
10	J.C. Penney Co.	74,568	90,721	(17.8)	17.5

Note: Dollars are in thousands. Source: Leading National Advertisers Multimedia Service, as compiled and published by Leading National Advertisers.

The advertising department is held accountable for the agency's performance and for the quality and effectiveness of the advertising. The advertising department usually has the power to approve or disapprove the agency's recommendations and ideas. Though the advertising department can usually reject an advertising recommendation proposed by an agency, in some cases approval or disapproval may come from the marketing or sales department or at higher levels of corporate management.

The latter is much more common in companies where advertising plays an important role in the success of the products. Such examples would include packaged-food companies, fragrances and cosmetics, fashion, and soft drinks. By contrast, in such businesses as heavy machinery, engineering, and financial institutions, decisions on marketing

Table 8.6 Top 10 magazine advertisers

Rank	Advertiser	Magazine expenditures 1988	1987	% chg	as % of co's '88 ad total
1	Philip Morris Cos.	$270,251	$271,178	(0.3)	13.1
2	General Motors Corp.	190,799	153,926	24.0	9.3
3	RJR Nabisco	131,463	105,674	24.4	6.4
4	Ford Motor Co.	125,532	125,529	0.0	6.1
5	Chrysler Corp.	104,527	100,433	4.1	5.1
6	Procter & Gamble Co.	79,279	79,501	(0.3)	3.9
7	American Telephone & Telegraph	66,193	76,270	(13.2)	3.2
8	Time Warner	64,989	53,029	22.6	3.2
9	Nestle SA	63,477	56,616	12.1	3.1
10	Grand Metropolitan PLC	59,545	54,948	8.4	2.9

Note: Dollars are in thousands. Source: Leading National Advertisers Multimedia Service, as compiled and published by Leading National Advertisers.

and advertising are generally left up to the experts who head these departments.

In some companies, the advertising departments can hire and fire agencies; in others, it can only recommend such action to top management. It is fair to say that the more important the advertising is to the success of the company's products, the more often top management is heavily involved in the final decision.

In companies that have more than one agency, the advertising department carries the responsibility to direct and coordinate the work of the different agencies. The department must make sure that advertising for each product is consistent and on target with company goals and image. Additionally, corporate media contracts must be coordinated and maintained to ensure that a given issue of a magazine does not carry too many advertisements for the company's products while the next issue carries none. The advertising department also must make sure that all scheduling is bulked so that the company gets the lowest possible frequency rate for its advertising. Most media offer rates that reduce the unit cost when six, twelve, or more advertisements are used by one advertiser in a given year.

The advertising department also controls the budget, which includes expenditures for time and space, production, and the internal costs of running the department—payroll, travel, phone, supplies, rent, and utilities—everything that is properly chargeable to the department.

Many advertising departments create and produce their own direct mail material and brochures, catalogs, packaging, and point-of-sale material, although this work is sometimes done by an agency or specialized outside supplier. Wherever such activities occur, it is the function of the advertising department to keep the work in harmony, and directed toward the same company goals, and consistent in tone and approach.

Job Opportunities in Corporate Advertising Departments

As one might expect, the structure in a corporate advertising department differs greatly from that of an advertising agency. In small companies, the advertising department is generally run by an advertising manager with the help of one or two assistants. In large corporations, the advertising department is likely to be headed by an advertising vice-president or a director of advertising who presides over separate advertising units, each under the direction of an advertising manager. In some cases, the department has its own research unit; in others, there is a separate research department that assists the advertising department.

Though advertising departments are set up differently than agencies, they employ similar kinds of people, often with identical qualifications and background. Although the work may be similar, the big difference, as we mentioned before, is that the advertising department can make the important final decisions and can commit the corporation's funds to do a job.

Some corporations have established house agencies whose structures, jobs, functions, and specialties are similar to those of an independent advertising agency. The only difference is that they work for just one client and are housed on the physical premises of the corporation, and are paid by the corporation. Because the people who work in these house agencies are on salary like other company employees, they are less concerned with profit and loss than are the employees of independently owned agencies.

BRAND MANAGEMENT

Brand or product management is the other principal area of corporate advertising. The brand manager concept was established in the 1930s by the giant packaged-goods corporation Procter and Gamble and has since been adopted by many companies, particularly those involved in food, packaged goods, and firms with many different products and brands.

Corporations that use the brand management system assign one person to a specific product (or product group). This person, often with his or her own staff, handles all of the work that needs to be done to advertise and market this product. In many ways, each product is treated as if it were a separate company—a kind of company within a company. In addition to advertising and sales promotion, the brand manager's responsibilities can include marketing strategy, business planning, profitability studies, and market research. Coordinating the advertising is only part of the job of the brand manager, but a no less important part. The life and death of a product can depend on the effectiveness of the advertising.

The brand manager works intimately with the account people and the creative people at the advertising agency. In the early stages of developing an advertising campaign, the brand manager plays a crucial role in the interaction with the agency. From the brand manager the agency gets a handle on the direction and goals of the client in regard to advertising for that particular product. Brand managers are heavily involved in the development of ideas presented by the agency early on, and later they may sit back and let the agency work its magic, checking on the work periodically to make sure it is in line with the company's objectives.

Success in brand management, though, has more to do with being a good businessperson than it does with being able to create advertising. A brand manager is really a heavily oriented marketing person, running a business within a business, selling one product with the advertising being one facet, but yet an important facet, of the business. A person in this position is also involved with product development, product improvement, packaging, marketing strategy, and a host of other details that evolve in the course of selling the product. This job is for someone with a talent for marketing and business *and* a head for advertising. If this is you, brand management could provide you with a challenging and rewarding career and a stepping stone to top level corporate management.

RETAIL

National retailers like J.C. Penney, Montgomery Ward, Wal-Mart, or Sears and large department stores all over the country provide another source of jobs outside of the advertising agency. Most retailers do their own advertising and rarely hire outside agencies. Since the bulk of their advertising is done in-house, talented professionals are needed to create and execute advertising for these retail marketers.

The world of retail hires a wide variety of advertising professionals, including copywriters, TV producers, art directors, media people, research people, and even traffic managers. Since ads need to be produced quickly and frequently, often designed to tie in with sales and in-store promotions, the advertising staff must be able to organize and maintain an efficient system of fast response in being able to put together the necessary advertising. Because of the speed required in producing retail advertising, quality is sometimes sacrificed, but getting the ad placed on time takes precedence over the finer points of good design. People who like a fast pace and who can work quickly and enjoy working under great pressure and daily deadlines are ideal candidates for jobs in retail advertising.

All in all, opportunities outside of the advertising agency are diverse and challenging. Often disregarded by those entering the advertising field, corporate and retail advertising jobs can lead to great personal and financial rewards that may not be found in advertising agencies. Remember to consider all the possibilities as you chart your career in advertising.

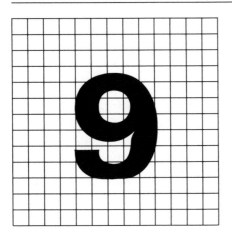

MEDIA SALES

Other positions that provide exciting careers in advertising include working for the advertising departments of media companies or working on their advertising sales staffs. The advertising departments of media firms function in a similar manner to advertising departments of corporations. Since media companies need advertising to impress and influence advertisers and advertising agencies, there's a great emphasis placed on highly creative and high-quality work. After all, these media companies want to sell space and time in their properties. As a result, media companies use every imaginative, creative, and innovative device to capture the attention of the advertising community. This includes space ads in the advertising press, sales presentations, slick research, premiums, and all sorts of clever direct mail.

Media firms are heavy users of direct mail because the ad agencies and advertisers whom they wish to influence are easy to identify and relatively few in number. This makes direct mail ideal for their purposes.

The function of the media sales department is to sell space in their publications or time on their stations or networks to agencies and advertisers. As a result, they call on advertisers and their agencies and find themselves totally immersed in the day-to-day world of advertising—dealing directly with company ad executives and calling upon agency media and account people. This selling is done on a one-to-one basis and through presentations to groups of agency and client people. Such presentations often involve the use of sophisticated audiovisual devices.

Today, media sales is a growth field and a strong area of opportunity. The industry is healthy and shows no sign of slowing down. Let's take a closer look at two important media sales areas—print and broadcast.

SELLING SPACE IN PRINT MEDIA

The Print Industry

Newspapers. The United States has about eighteen hundred daily newspapers and eighty-five hundred weekly newspapers, plus innumerable neighborhood papers, religious and ethnic papers, and specialized papers such as *The Wall Street Journal.*

More than sixty million people each day read at least part of a daily newspaper. Most newspapers are 65 percent advertising and currently account for over $4 billion worth of advertising a year. Newspapers made up approximately 13 percent of all advertising in 1986. The desirability of advertising in a specific paper depends on the rates, circulation, the market served, and the number of people who read it regularly. Advertisers and agencies gather the needed data from sources such as Standard Rate and Data Service (SRDS) and in discussions with newspaper advertising sales representatives.

Newspapers are the most timely of the print media because they are published so frequently—daily or at least weekly. Thus a department store ad for air conditioners can appear the morning of a forecasted heat wave.

Around 85 percent of all advertising appearing in newspapers is placed by local businesses. Sections within each newspaper attract advertisers whose products relate to the editorial content. Thus, cake mixes are advertised in the cooking or food section, homes and home improvement in the real estate section, and fishing tackle in the sports pages.

Newspapers carry classified and display advertising. Display ads will range from small ads up to as large as full page. Most display ads include illustrations. Classified ads, or want ads, often advertise jobs, real estate, used cars, or private goods for sale. Used car and some real estate classified ads may be large advertisements but most classified ads are only a few lines and seldom contain illustrations.

Magazines. Magazines are visually more attractive than newspapers and are generally published to serve a specific, or target audience. The editorial content of a magazine determines the audience it wishes to attract. Each magazine is edited to appeal to the needs, interests, or tastes of a particular cross-section of the public. *TV Guide,* which sells more copies than any other magazine, is edited for people with an interest in television programming and TV personalities. *Time* and *Newsweek* are current events magazines; *Tennis, Golf Digest, Working Mother,* and *Electronic Musician* are even more specialized.

Advertising people call these publications consumer magazines. Table 9.1 follows the continuing growth of the consumer magazine field since 1960.

Magazines that provide information and guidance about various highly specialized fields are called trade, business, or industrial magazines. Publications such as *Women's Wear Daily* or *Photographic Trade*

Table 9.1 Consumer magazine growth

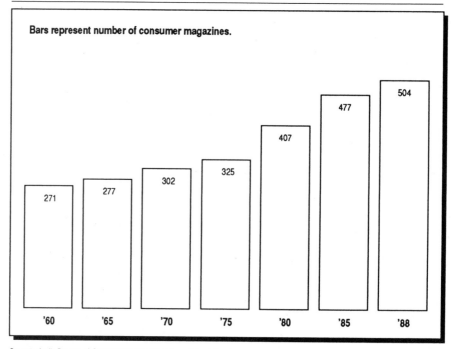

Bars represent number of consumer magazines.

271	277	302	325	407	477	504
'60	'65	'70	'75	'80	'85	'88

Source: Audit Bureau of Circulations. Reprinted from *Advertising Age.*

News and even a magazine called *Catalog Age* are classified as trade since they deal primarily with the news and changes in their respective fields. Closely related are business publications such as *Advertising Age, Adweek,* and *Business Marketing,* which serve the advertising profession, and publications like *Editor and Publisher* and *Publisher's Weekly,* which serve the publishing business. Industrial publications are generally more technical and would include titles such as *Electronic Products, Functional Photography,* and *Plastics Engineering.*

In addition to all of the above-mentioned national magazines, there is a growing group of publications edited for local consumption. Such magazines on the consumer side include statewide publications such as *Texas Monthly, Connecticut,* and *New Jersey.* There are also successful magazines that cater to highly affluent audiences on a local basis, such as *Palm Springs Life* for the resort community in California, and *North Shore Magazine,* which serves the wealthy suburban communities of Chicago. These local magazines are growing fast and are receiving more and more attention from national advertisers who need to advertise locally and prefer the more attractive appearance and environment of a magazine as opposed to a newspaper. Many national magazines have responded to this trend by now offering local metro editions that enable a national advertiser to place an ad in one or two local markets and not pay for the entire circulation.

Table 9.2 Magazine ad revenues

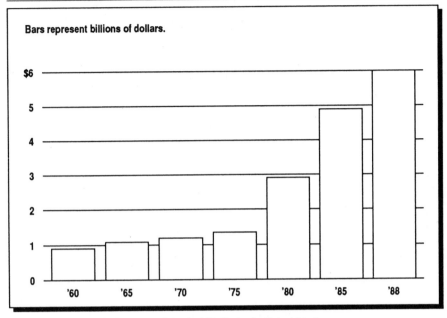

Bars represent billions of dollars.

Source: PIB/LNA Magazine Services, as compiled and published by Leading National Advertisers.

Nearly $6 billion were spent on magazine advertising in 1988—about 16 percent of all advertising dollars. Of this amount 60 percent was spent in consumer magazines and the other 40 percent in trade and business publications. The tables on the following pages illustrate the recent rapid increase in magazine ad revenues and ad-page sales.

Print Media Sales

The guaranteed minimum number of readers that a magazine or newspaper will deliver is a factor determining the "base rate" for ad space in that particular magazine or newspaper. Unlike TV time rates, print advertising rates are generally not negotiable. However, there is growing evidence that this situation is changing as advertisers and agencies are putting more pressure on media for price and merchandising concessions. Rates vary according to the size of ads and frequency of appearance of ads in a given twelve-month period. An advertiser who will run a six- or twelve-time schedule receives a better rate than the occasional one-time advertiser. Positions with higher visibility, such as the back cover and the inside front cover of a magazine, as well as the use of color, will add to the cost. Also, since there is no limit as to the available space that a publication can print, magazines and newspapers usually will try to sell as much advertising as possible.

Those working in print media sales, especially at magazines, must build their business with existing accounts and also develop new ac-

Table 9.3 Magazine ad-page sales

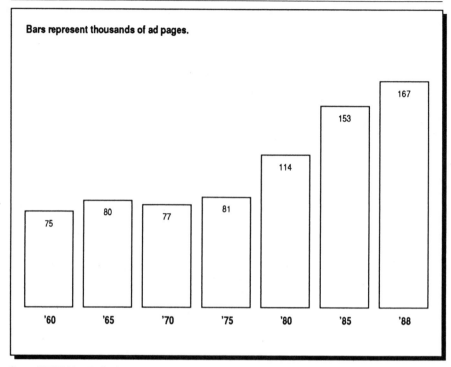

Source: PIB/LNA Magazine Services, as compiled and published by Leading National Advertisers.

counts. This is not as easy as it appears. A salesperson must become familiar with all aspects of the advertiser's business and must be able to offer suggestions to the advertiser on how to improve sales and increase market visibility through the use of his or her publication. A salesperson must take a personal interest in the client and the advertiser's success in order to build the client as an important advertiser. Acquiring new accounts is more difficult than maintaining existing accounts. A salesperson really has to sell that magazine to a new client and prove to that client that advertising in that magazine will be better than advertising elsewhere.

A great deal of information is gathered to support readership of successful magazines and newspapers. The ages, incomes, educational levels, occupations, buying habits, car ownership, and other characteristics of readers all influence advertising buying decisions. This information will influence the advertiser in the selection of one magazine over another and is the subject of constant debate among advertisers, agencies, and the media sales representatives. Equally important is editorial quality and environment, trends in circulation, the overall appearance of the publication, *and* its standing among the competition. The media sales representative performs the important task of providing advertisers and agencies with this vital information.

JOB OPPORTUNITIES IN THE PRINT MEDIA ADVERTISING DEPARTMENT

Account Manager or District Manager

The account manager or district manager is an ordinary salesperson with a fancy title who covers a specified geographic territory. The job calls for good old-fashioned sales work—maintaining old accounts, soliciting new ones, keeping up-to-date on accounts and competition and making lots of sales calls. These salespeople are the backbone of the media sales department and the economic success of the magazine or newspaper is based on their performance.

Group or Regional Manager

The group or regional manager serves as supervisor or sales manager to a given number of salespeople in a defined geographic area or branch office. Generally, this person double-teams with individual salespeople on tough prospects, larger accounts, and difficult sales situations. A group or regional manager is usually a proven salesperson who has moved up a notch.

Advertising Director

The advertising director is the head of the advertising sales department. This person acts as supervisor to the staff and oversees all areas of the department including promotion, advertising rate policies, forecasting and budgeting and of course the direction of the sales staff.

SELLING SPACE IN BROADCAST MEDIA

The Broadcast Industry

Television. By far the most visible, and most controversial, advertising medium is television. Since its beginnings around 1950, television has grown into the largest national advertising medium with revenue of nearly $20 billion in 1988. Network television commercials advertise products or services that have nationwide appeal and availability and which, for the most part, are financially within the reach of most people. By network TV we mean a number of television stations located in cities throughout the country that are affiliated with each other in order to carry the same program during a given time slot. Similarly, the same advertisements are generally shown with each program. Because of network television, each participating station can telecast a wider variety of shows and of better quality than they might produce on their own. And advertisers are assured of program consistency as their message is telecast across the country.

Local TV is used essentially by retailers, automobile dealers, department stores, banks, and other local businesses and merchants. More and more national advertisers use local TV to hype a product in a given market or to serve a special competitive need or satisfy a seasonal or geographic market need. Commercials may appear on locally produced shows or on nationally televised shows as local commercials.

The newest, and perhaps the fastest-growing, development in television is cable. Instead of choosing from among three to five channels, the viewer now may choose from as many as fifty or more channels. As a result, cable programming is expected to ultimately focus on the special interests of viewers so that a viewer may select channels devoted to specific interests. We are beginning to see this development taking shape with a twenty-four-hour news channel, sports channels, a country and western channel, a comedy channel, religious channels, and others. Because of this, advertisers can now select an environment in which the advertised product is more likely to attract the most interested buyers. For example, a brokerage house should reach better prospects for its services on Financial News Network (FNN) than it is likely to find on the Disney Channel.

A TV commercial may take the form of a thirty-second spot almost always televised with one immediately following another (a practice known as piggybacking). Commercials of ten and twenty seconds are also common. So-called station breaks, eight- to ten-second segments that appear between two programs, are another common form of commercials. Spots of one minute or longer, once very common, are now rare. On most television programs, commercials are spaced at ten- to twelve-minute intervals. Thus, the average prime-time network program has a total of about nine and one-half minutes of commercial advertising.

Advertisers, with input from their own advertising and marketing people and from their advertising agencies, are very selective in the shows they sponsor. Advertisers may select from sports events, comedies, dramas, or special events and will seek to create an atmosphere or setting that will successfully showcase the products they want to sell.

Radio. Although radio is primarily a local medium today, it reaches more people in more places and under more varied circumstances than any other medium. The majority of homes in this country have two or more radios. In addition, there are car radios, boat radios, portable radios, and radios with headphones for walkers and joggers. Today, automobile drivers and their passengers represent the largest segment of the radio audience.

Because of this, radio is used by national and local advertisers to promote goods and services that appeal to the masses and which are widely distributed and readily obtainable. For example, discount retailers are heavy radio advertisers; Tiffany's is not. About 6 percent of all advertising dollars—or about $2.3 billion in 1988—are spent on radio. Nearly 75 percent of this expenditure appears as local spot advertising.

Today, there are a limited number of network radio programs on the air, so most advertisers who wish to use radio coast-to-coast do so by buying spots on a station-by-station, city-by-city basis or by buying time

Table 9.4 50 leading media companies by revenue

Rank			Total media revenue		
1988	1987	Company, headquarters	1988	1987	% chg
1	1	Capital Cities/ABC, New York	$4,588.5	$4,256.2	7.8
2	2	Time Inc., New York	3,686.0	3,306.0	11.5
3	3	General Electric Co., Fairfield, Conn.	3,638.0	3,241.0	12.2
4	4	Gannett Co., Arlington, Va.	3,211.3	2,991.3	7.4
5	5	CBS Inc., New York	2,776.8	2,761.8	0.5
6	6	Times Mirror Co., Los Angeles	2,677.9	2,548.9	5.1
7	7	Advance Publications, Newark, N.J.	2,655.5	2,482.0	7.0
8	9	Knight-Ridder, Miami	2,077.1	1,943.9	6.9
9	10	Hearst Corp., New York	1,986.0	1,886.0	5.3
10	11	Tribune Co., Chicago	1,985.5	1,875.7	5.9
11	17	TCI, Denver	1,705.1	1,225.1	39.2
12	12	New York Times Co., New York	1,700.1	1,642.4	3.5
13	14	News Corp., Sydney	1,683.3	1,250.0	34.7
14	13	Cox Enterprises, Atlanta	1,578.2	1,463.6	7.8
15	15	Washington Post Co., Washington	1,305.6	1,240.3	5.3
16	19	Scripps Howard, Cincinnati	1,203.3	1,128.5	6.6
17	34	Thomson Corp., Toronto	1,126.0	973.4	15.7
18	20	Viacom International, New York	1,113.8	938.5	18.7
19	16	Dow Jones & Co., New York	973.1	987.7	(1.5)
20	24	Ingersoll Publications Co., Princeton, N.J.	645.0	609.0	5.9
21	25	Westinghouse Electric Corp., Pittsburgh	632.8	600.5	5.4
22	35	Continental Cablevision, Boston	622.0	442.0	40.7
23	29	Reader's Digest Assn., Pleasantville, N.Y.	600.4	522.2	15.0
24	30	Advo-System, Windsor, Conn.	589.0	520.5	13.2
25	22	MediaNews Group, Dallas	572.4	650.0	(11.9)
26	36	Turner Broadcasting System, Atlanta	537.6	436.4	23.2
27	NA	United Artists Entertainment Co., Denver	513.6	431.6	19.0
28	18	McGraw-Hill, New York	509.8	466.7	9.2
29	31	Affiliated Publications, Boston	506.5	472.8	7.1
30	38	Warner Communications, New York	496.4	425.0	16.8
31	56	Cablevision Systems Corp., Woodbury, N.Y.	493.5	299.5	64.8
32	33	Meredith Corp., Des Moines, Iowa	474.7	449.2	5.7
33	23	Storer Holdings, Miami	472.1	419.8	12.5
34	27	Harte-Hanks Communications, San Antonio, Texas	462.7	520.0	(11.0)
35	39	Media General, Richmond, Va.	449.4	424.1	6.0
36	42	Freedom Newspapers, Irvine, Calif.	432.0	392.0	10.2
37	48	Cahners Publishing Co., Newton, Mass.	420.0	340.0	23.5
38	37	Central Newspapers, Indianapolis	417.6	402.7	3.7
39	58	Comcast Corp., Bala Cynwyd, Pa.	404.1	286.8	40.9
40	41	Valassis Inserts, Livonia, Mich.	400.0	400.0	0.0
41	44	Pulitzer Publishing Co., St. Louis	391.0	367.3	6.5
42	43	A.H. Belo Corp., Dallas	385.4	381.7	1.0
43	46	Chronicle Publishing Co., San Francisco	384.0	357.0	7.6
44	45	Morris Communications, Augusta, Ga.	382.6	359.0	6.6
45	47	Copley Newspapers, La Jolla, Calif.	381.3	353.4	7.9
46	40	Multimedia Inc., Greenville, S.C.	374.0	352.6	6.1
47	32	Oklahoma Publishing Co., Oklahoma City	374.0	320.0	16.9
48	53	Hachette Publications, Paris	366.0	321.0	14.0
49	51	Landmark Communications, Norfolk, Va.	363.6	336.1	8.2
50	49	Gillett Holdings, Nashville	354.0	340.0	4.1

Note: Dollar amounts are in millions. Source: *Advertising Age.*

Table 9.5 Media companies ranked by newspaper revenue

Rank 1988	Rank 1987	Company	Newspaper revenue 1988	Newspaper revenue 1987	% chg	All media revenue 1988	Newspaper revenue % all media	Top newspaper by daily circulation Newspaper	Circulation 3/31/89	'89–'88 % chg
1	1	Gannett Co.	$2,594.3	$2,432.5	6.7	$3,211.3	80.8	USA Today	1,656,467	4.4
2	2	Times Mirror Co.	1,997.7	1,995.9	0.1	2,677.9	74.6	Los Angeles Times	1,119,840	(1.2)
3	3	Knight-Ridder Newspapers	1,917.4	1,844.6	3.9	2,077.1	92.3	Detroit Free Press	629,275	(2.9)
4	4	Advance Publications	1,681.1	1,601.0	5.0	2,655.5	63.3	(Newark, N.J.) Star-Ledger	458,049	(0.4)
5	5	Tribune Co.	1,561.7	1,465.7	6.5	1,985.5	78.7	New York Daily News	1,230,186	(4.1)
6	6	New York Times Co.	1,380.1	1,348.6	2.3	1,700.1	81.2	New York Times	1,117,376	3.6
7	7	Dow Jones & Co.	937.1	948.7	(1.2)	973.1	96.3	Wall Street Journal	1,931,410	(4.6)
8	8	Scripps Howard	839.7	818.2	2.6	1,203.3	69.8	Rocky Mountain News	365,493	2.4
9	9	Cox Enterprises	739.0	710.6	4.0	1,578.2	46.8	(Atlanta) Constitution	282,442	3.6
10	10	Hearst Corp.	689.0	650.0	6.0	1,986.0	34.7	Houston Chronicle	427,844	3.9

Notes: Dollars are in millions. Ratings given for 1987 in this table are based on figures restated or estimated in 1988, some of which are pro forma. Only companies among the 100 leading media companies are ranked in this table. Sources: Newspaper revenues are *Advertising Age* estimates. Daily circulation from Audit Bureau of Circulations Fas-Fax Report, March 31, 1989. Percent change on circulation computed from March 31, 1988 figures, not shown. Reprinted from *Advertising Age.*

through the large radio networks such as Westwood One (owners of NBC Radio and Mutual Broadcasting) or ABC Cap Cities.

An advertiser can also be selective in choosing an audience that is more likely to be interested in the advertised product or service. For example, early morning and late afternoon broadcasts are listened to by people driving to and from work. Since these are heard by automobile owners, advertisers selling cars and products related to the interests of businesspeople are more likely to do well.

Another consideration is the use of radio in relationship to the selection of stations according to their programming. A station featuring

Table 9.6 Media companies ranked by magazine revenue

Rank 1988	Rank 1987	Company	Magazine revenue 1988	Magazine revenue 1987	% chg	All media revenue 1988	Magazine revenue % all media	Top magazine by gross ad revenue Magazine	Ad revenue 1988	'88–'87 % chg
1	1	Time Inc.	$1,752.0	$1,621.0	8.1	$3,686.0	47.5	Time	$349.7	6.4
2	2	Hearst Corp.	919.0	873.0	5.3	1,986.0	46.3	Good Housekeeping	129.3	(2.4)
3	3	Advance Publications	745.0	678.0	9.9	2,655.5	28.1	Parade	266.5	19.2
4	5	Reader's Digest Assn.	600.4	522.2	15.0	600.4	100.0	Reader's Digest	114.0	6.3
5	4	Thomson Corp.	596.0	528.0	12.9	1,126.0	52.9	Medical Economics	25.3	3.3
6	13	News Corp.	509.6	332.8	53.1	1,683.3	30.3	TV Guide	335.4	1.3
7	8	Cahners Publishing Co.	420.0	340.0	23.5	420.0	100.0	Restaurants & Institutions	39.7	(0.5)
8	6	McGraw-Hill	413.7	377.0	9.7	509.8	81.1	Business Week	227.3	4.5
9	7	Capital Cities/ABC	370.0	374.8	(1.3)	4,588.5	8.1	W	27.1	30.9
10	11	Hachette Group	366.0	321.0	14.0	366.0	100.0	Woman's Day	115.6	0.1

Notes: Dollars are in millions. Ratings given for 1987 in this table are based on figures restated or estimated in 1988, some of which are pro forma. Only companies among the 100 leading media companies are included in this ranking. Sources: Newspaper revenues are *Advertising Age* estimates. Ad revenue from Publishers Information Bureau. Percent change computed on ad revenue from 1987 figures, not shown. Reprinted from *Advertising Age.*

Table 9.7 Media companies ranked by TV revenue

Rank 1988	Rank 1987	Company	TV revenue 1988	TV revenue 1987	% chg	All media revenue 1988	TV revenue % all media	Top TV station by average households reached Station	Avg. h'hlds 2/89	'88–'87 % chg
1	1	General Electric Co.	$3,638.0	$3,241.0	12.2	$3,638.0	100.0	KNBC, NBC, Los Angeles	321,613	0.2
2	2	Capital Cities/ABC	3,306.3	3,028.7	9.2	4,588.5	72.1	WABC, ABC, New York	532,935	(18.4)
3	3	CBS Inc.	2,612.1	2,611.4	0.0	2,776.8	94.1	WCBS, CBS, New York	401,432	(8.8)
4	4	News Corp.	620.0	576.8	7.5	1,683.3	36.8	WNYW, FOX, New York	346,062	4.8
5	5	Westinghouse Electric Corp.	521.2	500.5	4.1	632.8	82.4	KYW, NBC, Philadelphia	185,338	(0.2)
6	6	Tribune Co.	378.6	366.2	3.4	1,985.5	19.1	WPIX, IND, New York	256,086	12.8
7	7	Gillett Holdings	354.0	340.0	4.1	354.0	100.0	WJBK, CBS, Detroit	123,711	(7.9)
8	8	Gannett Co.	305.5	277.6	10.1	3,211.3	9.5	WUSA, CBS, Washington	136,569	(6.6)
9	9	Cox Enterprises	286.6	266.8	7.4	1,578.2	18.2	WSB, ABC, Atlanta	133,864	0.9
10	10	Hearst Corp.	234.7	236.8	(0.9)	1,986.0	11.8	WCVB, ABC, Boston	158,813	(13.6)

Notes: Dollars are in millions. Ratings given for 1987 in this table are based on figures restated or estimated, some of which are pro forma. Only companies among the 100 leading media companies are ranked in this table. Sources: TV revenues are *Advertising Age* estimates. Average households from A.C. Nielsen, Feb. 1989 ratings and number of households. Percent change on households from Feb. 1988 figures, not shown. Reprinted from *Advertising Age*.

country music will have a loyal and definitive audience that appeals to advertisers who identify with that type of consumer. Some stations aim at reaching special ethnic groups; others are beamed to identifiable age and consumer groups. The products advertised on these stations are the ones likely to appeal to the tastes of such listeners.

Broadcast Media Sales

The big difference between selling space in print and selling time in a broadcast is that broadcast rates are highly negotiable and no two advertisers can be on the same station on the same program in the same exact time slot. As a result there is a lot of jockeying about. The price of a ten-second spot will vary considerably from the number one TV show to a time slot for a less popular show at an off-hour time. And since the popularity of programming changes constantly, so do the advertising rates.

When local stations expect to sell time to national advertisers, they do so through national rep firms. These firms are located in major advertising centers and they interact with advertising agency spot buyers. A rep firm can be thought of as the local station's agent, or representative in the marketplace, or as the middleman between the local stations and the advertisers. They help to match the station's available time with the advertiser's needs. Working for a radio or television rep firm calls for an added amount of salesmanship due to the fact that you must not only sell the advertiser time, but you often need to sell or negotiate with the station to accept your advertiser's commercials in the time slots they want. Obviously there is a lot of interest among advertisers to run their commercials in prime slots and in conjunction with special events. It is a challenging, and at times stressful, work.

Table 9.8 Media companies ranked by cable revenue

Rank 1988	1987	Company	Cable revenue 1988	1987	% chg	All media revenue 1988	Cable revenue % all media	MSO property (if applicable) Cable	Basic subscribers	Count date
1	1	Time Inc.	$1,934.0	$1,685.0	14.8	$3,686.0	52.5	ATC Corp.	3,900,000	12/88
2	2	TCI	1,705.1	1,225.1	39.2	1,705.1	100.0	TCI	5,977,790	12/88
3	3	Viacom International	972.6	806.4	20.6	1,113.8	87.3	Viacom Cablevision	1,114,500	12/88
4	4	Continental Cablevision	622.0	442.0	40.7	622.0	100.0	Continental Cablevision	2,302,000	12/88
5	5	Turner Broadcasting System	537.6	436.4	23.2	537.6	100.0			
6	6	United Artists Entertainment Co.	513.6	431.6	19.0	513.6	100.0	UAE	1,339,729	10/88
7	10	Cablevision Systems Corp.	493.5	299.5	64.8	493.5	100.0	Cablevision Systems Corp.	1,140,014	11/88
8	8	Storer Holdings	472.1	419.8	12.5	472.1	100.0	SCI Holdings	1,516,623	12/88
9	7	Cox Enterprises	471.8	425.0	11.0	1,578.2	29.9	Cox Cable Communications	1,465,245	12/88
10	9	Warner Communications	456.4	387.0	17.9	496.4	91.9	Warner Cable	1,488,720	12/88

Notes: Dollars are in millions. Ratings given for 1987 in this table are based on figures restated or estimated in 1988, some of which are pro forma. Only 100 leading media cos. are ranked in this table. Cable revenues are *Advertising Age* estimates. Total number of basic subscribers in the MSO are from Cabletelevision Advertising Bureau, Cable TV Fact Book, 1989 edition. Reprinted from *Advertising Age*.

Often, in the network TV arena, bids are solicited by advertisers and/ or agencies for time on a particular network, and the salesperson that can put together the best package for the advertiser will get the business. Sometimes, the advertiser will establish a set budget to spend on advertising and will ask a network to come up with the best possible package within the stated budget. The proposal will include pricing, time and dates, and the particular programs for the campaign. The proposal with the best mix of programming, price, and available time will usually land the business.

TV network sales is a huge business, but there are a limited number of positions in network TV media sales. Landing a job in this area without a successful sales record is extremely difficult.

Media sales in the local market for local radio and TV stations is usually handled by the station's own sales staff. The local ads that run on these stations are negotiated and sold by the sales staff and usually run on local programs, though they sometimes appear in the station breaks on network or syndicated shows.

Besides the advertising sales staff, all TV networks and many individual stations have advertising departments that work on promoting advertising sales and building audiences. Either working in tandem with their own ad agency or working separately, these advertising departments handle the ads to promote the shows for a new season, promotions, and publicity. These advertising departments are not a part of the media sales department. They offer an excellent opportunity to work in advertising with advertisers and with advertising agencies.

JOB OPPORTUNITIES IN BROADCAST MEDIA SALES

Sales Planner

This position is basically administrative, and may include such duties as computer work, basic research, maintenance of files, and answering phones. It is a starting point for many people who want to break into the business.

Sales Assistant

In network TV and with large stations, this is generally the next step up from sales planner. A person in this position prepares proposals to serve the needs of advertisers. This is a job that provides an excellent opportunity to learn how to prepare schedules and to learn about the industry.

Account Executive or Sales Representative

On a small station or at a rep firm, this is often an entry-level position. This is typically the only sales job one can land right out of college, as other broadcast sales jobs usually require experience. Account executives and sales representatives negotiate and sell the broadcast time. They have heavy contact with advertisers and advertising agencies. An account executive must be acutely aware of what is happening day to day with the network stations and with competition.

WHAT IT TAKES TO BE A GOOD MEDIA SALESPERSON

The job of media sales representative requires specialized personal attributes and talents. Sales representatives should be personable, highly articulate, persuasive, and extremely knowledgeable about their media and competitors, particularly as they relate to the needs and sales objectives of advertisers and prospects. What this means is that, like a good agency account person, a top-flight media sales representative should devote a great deal of time and effort to analyzing and understanding the advertiser's business—the problems, opportunities, and competition. The surest way to be an unsuccessful advertising sales representative is to approach an advertiser or agency with a briefcase full of solutions to problems that do not exist. In any field of advertising, it is important to approach each prospect or assignment with as much information and background on the advertiser as is humanly possible. Always be prepared. It will lead to success and save a lot of embarrassment and grief.

Other Opportunities

In addition to advertising sales opportunities with media firms there are a number of independent advertising sales rep firms. They offer excellent careers for people who enjoy both sales and advertising. Generally they specialize in one of the four media areas discussed in this chapter. The larger firms offer on-the-job training and good supervision and guidance. Working for such firms offers diversification since you generally work on more than one magazine or newspaper, or in the case of broadcast, on a variety of stations. One such firm in magazine representation is Pattis/3M, a division of the Advertising Services Group of the giant 3M company. This particular unit of 3M employs a staff of over fifty salespeople working out of six company offices nationwide and overseas. A back-up staff of comparable size provides the salespeople with market research, secretarial, accounting, and general management.

Because people working in media sales are so close to advertisers and advertising agencies, they usually develop good contacts with people within these organizations. And since many of the skills needed in the two professions are similar, working in advertising sales can be either a valuable first step in an advertising career for a lifetime profession. Developing skills in advertising sales work can lead to a number of positions, including advertising director of a radio station or TV network. In the print field, it may lead to top-level positions such as publisher of a large magazine. Advertising sales is the basis for most income for the media and being successful in this area can lead to excellent personal and financial rewards.

Finally, let's take a look at where the jobs are in media sales. Tables 9.4 through 9.8 on the previous pages list the fifty leading media companies by revenue and the ten leading media companies in the following areas—newspaper, magazine, TV, and cable. As you can see, it's a field with endless opportunities.

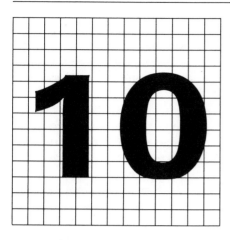

OTHER CAREERS IN ADVERTISING

In addition to the jobs available in the country's eight thousand advertising agencies, many other employment opportunities exist for those interested in working in advertising. We have already discussed the opportunities available in the fields of corporate advertising and media sales. Now, let's take a look at four more areas related to advertising—public relations, publicity, sales promotion, and direct mail. A job in any of these areas can provide a lifetime career with opportunity for advancement, security, and personal satisfaction.

PUBLIC RELATIONS

Public relations and publicity are closely related to advertising. Both try to create good and lasting impressions of a product, idea, or service to the public. Some agencies even have their own public relations departments. On the client side, public relations people may work on the staff of the corporate advertising department. Despite the labels, however, in these situations the people almost always function as publicists. True public relations (PR) is just what the term implies—the art of relating the affairs of an organization and of communicating a favorable impression of that organization to the public. The art of having good public relations was once described as being 95 percent what you do and 5 percent what you say. As a result, public relations counselors and consultants advise their clients on their actions as well as on their words. In doing so, they generally deal with the very top people in the companies they serve. Thus, they are required to have a sense of what people outside the organization are thinking and how they are likely to react to a given act by the company.

Public relations professionals need to be mature and have a good perception of what will interest the public. And like advertising professionals, public relations professionals must combine an ability to sell ideas to the media and the public with the skill of communicating well in writing.

The principal job of many public relations departments is to write day-to-day press releases on matters concerning the company, from the company president's position on financial matters to perhaps the appointment of a new director of personnel. Press releases are created on new products, changes in corporate policy, and on corporate issues. Writing simple press releases is often one of the first jobs given to people just starting out in the business. Later, as they acquire more writing and public relations skills, professionals may be asked to write speeches for corporate officers or feature articles for publications and reports that represent the organization to shareholders and others.

Other aspects of public relations include placement of press releases and feature stories with the media and arranging for interviews and personal appearances for spokespeople of the company. Just as in advertising, public relations personnel must select appropriate media, whether newspapers, magazines, radio, or television, that will best convey their message to targeted audiences. However, unlike advertising, identifying the media is not enough. Public relations professionals must convince editors, columnists, talk show directors, and others, that the story they want to place is timely, accurate, and of interest to their audiences.

Just as advertising account executives must work with clients to convince them of the desirability of certain advertisements, the public relations professional must work with clients to convince them how to present material, and at the same time, work with outside media to use the material.

PUBLICITY

Publicity and public relations differ from advertising in various ways. Advertising is written and placed exactly as the advertiser wants, since the client pays for it. Publicity, on the other hand, and its use and final wording are determined by the editorial staff of the media to which it is submitted. In short, the advertiser controls the advertisement, and the media controls publicity.

Publicity obviously involves risks not present in advertising. The media may completely change a story by the way in which it is rewritten. On the other hand, publicity does provide free exposure for the product or service. And of great importance, skillfully prepared publicity material appearing as editorial matter adds credibility to the product or service.

Publicity can take many forms and has many uses. The following is only a sampling of the most common activities.

New products or services. In areas in which there is genuine public interest, many news and picture releases appear in print almost verbatim as submitted. Examples of general interest would be the introduction of a new television set or a new model of car. The real challenge comes in getting coverage for items, such as tires, paint, or floor wax, with low intrinsic public interest value.

Product demonstrations. Many household and personal care products lend themselves to demonstration on TV daytime talk shows, and publicity like the announcement of an exciting new Hollywood film may find its way onto national evening news programs.

Case histories. Some products lend themselves to more comprehensive coverage. These might include a major development in home computers or a cure for a fatal disease.

Newsworthy promotional devices. Some products are of sufficient interest to the masses to make it easy to create a special event. Advance fashion news featuring a new collection of a top designer is a good example of what can be made into a major publicity event.

Use of prominent personalities. Some products lend themselves to endorsement by public figures who are in the news. Of course, these people expect to be paid for their endorsement.

Contrived events. These promotions are usually designed to capture big audiences at sporting events and other activities that draw large crowds. The opportunities are endless, but can include the Goodyear blimp or "Miller Beer Night" at a baseball game.

Day-to-day activities. Publicity involves considerable work that is not necessarily glamorous. These day-to-day activities include grinding out releases on the election or promotion of an executive, the opening or closing of a plant or the appointment of an employee to the chairmanship of some civic or charity organization.

Personal publicity. This sort of work is designed to enhance the reputation of a business client. It may involve ghostwriting speeches, interviews, the preparation of feature articles, or arranging for the personality to appear as a guest on a television or radio show.

Financial PR. This is a highly specialized form of public relations which deals with the placement of financial news and reports, including glorifying the company to shareholders and the financial community. This type of writing is not easy as the information must influence hard-nosed investment people and comply with labor unions and federal regulatory bodies. A good understanding of business and finance is needed.

Qualifications

Top-flight publicity people need a developed promotional flair, advanced writing skills, keen perception of what is newsworthy, and good contacts within the media. In some fields, technical knowledge is also required.

SALES PROMOTION

Sales promotion is yet another advertising-related field that shows great potential. Jobs in sales promotion can be found within advertising agencies, specialized sales promotion companies, and within corporate marketing departments.

Sales promotion promotes products and services through the use of sweepstakes, brochures, giveaways, point-of-purchase displays, packaging, direct mail, and even offbeat items such as T-shirts, bumper stickers, and posters. In sales promotion, as in publicity and PR, there is no commission to be earned by an advertising agency. Income is earned by charges for creative services and fees based on time and often on what the traffic will bear. The following table lists the top services, or the different activities, of sales promotion agencies.

Table 10.1 Top services of sales promotion agencies

Service	Total revenues 1988	1987	% chg
Consulting, planning, strategy	99,742	80,540	23.8
Production	40,377	39,223	2.9
Point-of-purchase	39,726	29,658	33.9
Creative services	31,792	26,894	18.2
Direct marketing	23,454	21,355	9.8
Sweepstakes, games, contests	20,733	20,705	0.1
Graphics	13,560	12,965	4.6
Incentives	12,536	12,919	(3.0)
Audio, visual	11,427	9,200	24.2
Event marketing	11,108	6,117	81.6
Advertising, media	9,577	8,514	12.5
Premiums	9,179	9,294	(1.2)
Fulfillment	8,243	5,275	56.3
Other	38.777	33,251	16.6
Subtotal service revenues reported*	370,230	315,911	17.2
Total revenues (all agencies)	498,550	404,315	23.3

Notes: Dollars are in thousands, 1987 figures are *Advertising Age* estimates. *Total includes only agencies that broke out services.
Source: *Advertising Age* survey.

Table 10.2 Top full-service sales promotion agencies

Rank	Agency, headquarters	Total revenues	
		1988	1987
1	American Consulting Corp. (FKB), New York	$24,300	$25,500
2	D.L. Blair Corp., Garden City, N.Y.	24,200	22,500
3	Frankel & Co., Chicago	19,600	14,000
4	Lintas: Marketing Communications, New York	18,315	15,923
5	Sales Aides International, Melrose Park, Pa.	16,555	9,851
6	CCG/TCA, Greenwich, Conn.	16,425	10,653
7	Einson Freeman, Paramus, N.J.	16,000	9,500
8	Promotion Group, Irvine, Calif.	15,430	12,050
9	Sage Worldwide Promotions, New York	14,108	7,105
10	Comart-KLP, New York	13,700	12,900

Note: Dollars are in thousands. Source: *Advertising Age*

In the advertising agency setting, sales promotion may be handled by the client's regular team of account managers, copywriters, art directors, and production people. Sometimes advertising agencies will be hired to do sales promotion for a particular client or project. Sales promotion jobs on the corporate side involve functions similar to those on the agency side—planning, designing, and producing such materials.

Besides the job opportunities available in agencies and corporations, there are a growing number of independent sales promotion firms that offer jobs in this field. Table 10.2 lists the top independent sales promotion agencies. Take note that almost all of them report an increase in revenues from 1987 to 1988.

Sales promotion looks to be one of the fastest-growing advertising-related areas in the coming years. In fact, *Advertising Age* calls sales promotion "marketing's rising star" and notes that sales promotion is growing at a rate two and a half times faster than general advertising. Jobs in sales promotion firms tend to be found in the eastern United States, but there are opportunities throughout the country. If you're looking for an exciting, growth field, sales promotion may be for you.

DIRECT MAIL

Direct mail advertising brings advertising directly into the home and office. It is one of the fastest-growing areas in the field of advertising. Direct mail appears in many sizes, shapes, and forms. At one end of the spectrum is what the public commonly refers to as junk mail, which is impersonal mail simply addressed to "occupant." At the other end of the spectrum are personalized letters addressed to the recipient by name and bearing an authentic signature. Today, telemarketing, or the selling of products and services over the phone is helping to expand this field into what is known as direct marketing.

Table 10.3 Top U.S.-based direct-response agencies by volume

Rank	Agency, headquarters	Total direct response volume 1988	1987
1	Ogilvy & Mather Direct, New York	$272,000	$260,000
2	Wunderman Worldwide, New York	266,133	260,000
3	Rapp Collins Marcoa, New York, N.Y.	236,300	218,600
4	Foote, Cone & Belding/Direct, Los Angeles	169,000	150,600
5	Direct Marketing Group, New York	136,700	134,700
6	Grey Direct International, New York	108,000	92,500
7	Kobs & Draft Advertising, Chicago	90,215	85,278
8	Barry Blau & Partners, Fairfield, Conn.	85,304	72,335
9	Chapman Stone & Adler, New York	83,646	74,919
10	Devon Direct Marketing & Advertising, Malvern, Pa.	66,200	53,000

Note: Dollars are in thousands. Source: *Advertising Age*

Direct mail may be in the form of letters, postcards, envelopes with various stuffers, booklets, catalogs, or brochures. Because of computers, people working in direct mail can select names from mailing lists by every possible classification, including zip code, income, type of job, type of previous purchases, amount of purchase, and life-style patterns. More and more marketers, both local and national, use direct mail to sell goods and services.

Direct mail is generally more expensive than other major media. The cost to reach a thousand people is used as a standard measure. Though the return rate of people responding to direct mailing is often as low as a fraction of 1 percent, direct mail is particularly valuable to many advertisers because its response is the most truly measurable of any form of advertising. As a result of continuous testing of offers and different copy approaches, the responsiveness of different lists can be predicted with surprising accuracy.

Direct mail and direct marketing were once the "poor sisters" of the advertising industry, but no longer. Today, this is a hot field and many agencies have even started their own direct marketing divisions. Table 10.3 lists the top ten direct response billers according to *Advertising Age*.

Direct mail is a great way to break into the advertising business, especially if you are an aspiring copywriter. Due to the recent boom in the business, there are many jobs available—many more than in the general advertising areas.

EMPLOYMENT AND ADVANCEMENT

The advertising job market should continue to grow with an expanded economy. It is an industry that offers great opportunity for those who have creative minds and the willingness to work. As table 11.1 indicates, the number of people in advertising and the number of advertising agencies increased from 1987 to 1988. These figures reflect the continued growth of the industry.

WHERE THE JOBS ARE

In chapter 8, we learned of the surprising number of job opportunities in corporate advertising. Here we will examine the job opportunities on the agency side, where most young people turn for their start in a career in advertising. There are many agencies across the country and throughout the world, from huge conglomerates to smaller shops. Needless to say, all of these many agencies are vying for the advertising dollar. Whether you would feel more comfortable at a large or small agency, opportunities exist, but you must be clever to land the job of your choice.

Table 11.1 Total agency personnel and facilities

	Top 25 agencies		Top 100 agencies		Top 500 agencies	
	1988	**1987**	**1988**	**1987**	**1988**	**1987**
Worldwide personnel	104,250	96,665	117,318	109,559	135,483	126,974
Domestic personnel	43,226	41,757	56,038	54,420	74,203	71,835
Worldwide offices	2,149	1,850	2,349	2,044	2,877	2,566
Domestic offices	476	455	664	637	1,192	1,159

Source: *Advertising Age* survey.

Table 11.2 Top 50 U.S.-based agencies by gross income

Rank 1988	1987		Agency, headquarters	Worldwide gross income 1988	1987
1	1	✔	Young & Rubicam**, New York	$757.6	$735.5
2	2		Saatchi & Saatchi Advertising Worldwide, New York	740.5	685.3
3	3		Backer Splelvogel Bates Worldwide, New York	689.8	600.7
4	6	✔	McCann-Erickson Worldwide, New York	656.8	512.5
5	13	✔	FCB-Publicis, Chicago/Paris	653.3	518.5
6	5	✔	Ogilvy & Mather Worldwide, New York	635.2	563.9
7	4	✔	BBDO Worldwide, New York	585.9	549.7
8	7	✔	J. Walter Thompson Co., New York	559.3	487.6
9	8	✔	Lintas: Worldwide, New York	537.6	417.9
10	11	✔	Grey Advertising, New York	432.8	369.2
11	9	✔	D'Arcy Masius Benton & Bowles, New York	428.7	371.3
12	10	✔	Leo Burnett Co., Chicago	428.4	369.2
13	12	✔	DOB Needham Worldwide, New York	399.9	368.5
14	14	✔	HDM, New York (33% Y&R)	279.0	204.0
15	16	✔	NW Ayer, New York	185.2	166.1
16	15	✔	Bozell, Jacobs, Kenyon & Eckhardt, New York	179.2	185.2
17	17		Wells, Rich, Greene*, New York	117.3	107.0
18	18	✔	Scali McCabe Sloves, New York	107.0	93.1
19	19	✔	Ketchum Communications, Pittsburgh	105.9	88.1
20	23		Campbell-Mithun-Esty, Minneapolis, Minn. (BSBW)	105.6	99.9
21	21		TBWA Advertising, New York	97.4	74.6
22	20	✔	Ogilvy & Mather Direct Response, New York (O&M)	97.0	84.0
23	22	✔	Ross Roy Group, Bloomfield Hills, Mich	85.2	71.3
24	38		Della Femina, McNamee WCRS, New York	84.4	78.9
25	24	✔	Wunderman Worldwide, New York (Y&R)	68.6	62.1
26	25		Chiat/Day, Venice, Calif.	65.0	52.5
27	26	✔	Tracy-Locke, Dallas (BBDO)	54.5	47.3
28	29	✔	Hill, Holiday, Connors, Cosmopulos, Boston	50.2	43.4
29	27	✔	Lowe Marschalk, New York	45.6	45.6
30	35		AC&R Advertising, New York	44.2	45.3
31	31		Laurence, Charles, Free & Lawson*, New York	43.3	43.2
32	30		McCaffrey & McCall, New York (S&SAW)	41.9	41.2
33	33		W.B. Doner & Co., Southfield, Mich/Baltimore	41.9	40.6
34	37		Admarketing Inc., Los Angeles	40.4	36.0
35	34		Jordan, McGrath, Case & Taylor, New York	38.5	38.4
36	40		Earle Palmer Brown Cos., Bethesda, Md.	36.2	33.1
37	42	✔	Medicus Intercon International, New York (DMB&B)	35.5	32.0
38	36		Ally & Gargano, New York	34.4	37.2
39	44	✔	Bernard Hodes Group, New York (DDB)	32.8	28.1
40	45		Levine, Huntley, Schmidt & Beaver, New York	32.1	26.9

(continued on next page)

Table 11.2 lists the top 50 agencies based in the United States by gross income. These are the largest agencies in this country, and many of them employ several thousand employees. Use this chart as a guide when looking for employment at a larger agency. Success breeds success, and

Table 11.2 Top 50 U.S.-based agencies by gross income (Continued)

Rank 1988	Rank 1987		Agency, headquarters	Worldwide gross income 1988	Worldwide gross income 1987
41	51	✔	Telephone Marketing Programs, New York	$ 31.4	$ 23.2
42	48	✔	Sudler & Hennessey, New York (Y&R)	29.5	26.8
43	47	✔	Ammirati & Puris, New York	28.0	25.5
44	28	✔	Doremus & Co., New York (BBDO)	26.5	28.0
45	46		Direct Marketing Group, New York	26.1	25.6
46	43		Tatham-Laird & Kudner, Chicago	26.0	28.9
47	80		Kobs & Draft Advertising, Chicago (BSBW)	25.0	12.8
48	41	✔	LGFE Inc., New York	24.6	31.8
49	50		Nationwide Advertising Service, Cleveland	24.1	20.4
50	56		Warwick Advertising, New York	24.0	21.0

Notes: Dollars are in millions. Initials in parentheses indicate the parent company in which the subsidiaries' figures are included.
✔ Indicates that the agency received signature of an independent accountant verifying figures supplied to AA.
 * indicates that gross income and/or total volume figures are AA estimates.
 ** Y&R's 1987 totals include nonmedia-related gross income and billings figures eliminated from 1988 results.
Source: *Advertising Age*.

chances are many of these firms need fresh, new ideas and new people at this very moment.

The most successful agencies have the pressure to continue to grow and expand. While they are in a growth mode, agencies offer greater job opportunities and chances for advancement, but it also holds true that with a loss of major accounts they can slide down quickly. Table 11.3 demonstrates how U.S.-based agencies proliferate the international advertising scene.

Mega Groups

A mega group is an advertising conglomerate that deals also in nonmedia advertising and other areas, such as consulting, public relations, and

Table 11.3 Top 10 agencies worldwide/1988

Rank	Agency	Worldwide gross income
1	Dentsu Inc.	$1,229
2	Young & Rubicam	758
3	Saatchi & Saatchi Advertising Worldwide	740
4	Backer Spielvogel Bates Worldwide	690
5	McCann-Erickson Worldwide	657
6	FCB-Publicis	653
7	Ogilvy & Mather Worldwide	635
8	BBDO Worldwide	586
9	J. Walter Thompson Co.	559
10	Lintas: Worldwide	538

Note: Dollars are in millions. Source: *Advertising Age*.

direct response. Mega groups are typically worldwide operations that started out as advertising agencies and then branched out into other service areas as their advertising business became more and more successful. It is possible to become employed at a large agency or mega group in a nonagency type of job, due to the wide range of positions offered by these companies.

Table 11.4 shows the top mega groups by worldwide gross income, and table 11.5 shows the top mega groups minus their nonmedia advertising.

In order to see what a mega group looks like on the inside, let's take a closer look at Saatchi & Saatchi PLC in table 11.6, as it appeared at the height of its activities in the late 1980s.

Here, we can see how the company is divided into two main branches: Communications and Consulting. The areas associated with advertising agencies in general, such as advertising, public relations, and sales promotion, are found under the Communications wing. Those areas not normally found in advertising agencies, such as marketing and sales, litigation services, and technology development, fall under Consulting. In larger operations like Saatchi & Saatchi, a greater variety of possible employment opportunities are available. Opportunities for attorneys and personnel managers interested in working in an advertising agency environment can be found within many of these mega groups.

The job possibilities here are great and varied, but before we can make it to Saatchi & Saatchi or Young & Rubicam, we must take the first steps.

GETTING STARTED

Before applying for your first job, decide what you want to do or be in advertising—the kind of job that would work out best for you and *for your employer*. The emphasis here is important, because you must never forget that the job hunter must always focus on what he or she has to offer that is valuable to the prospective employer. In simple terms, the question to be addressed is, "What can I do for you?" *not* "What can you do for me?"

In deciding what type of advertising job suits you best you should try to analyze your strengths and weaknesses. What do you do well? What kind of useful and applicable experience have you had? What sort of things do you like to do and why? What do you dislike doing and why? Are you impatient with details? Are you inclined to be analytical? Are you at ease with people, or do you prefer to stay in the background?

This kind of self-analysis is useful and not nearly as difficult as it sounds. But it does take deliberate thought and a totally honest appraisal of yourself. When you have completed the self-analysis, you will be in a position to zero in on the kind of job for which you are best qualified and at which you are most likely to succeed. You may also find that you have weaknesses that you need to overcome. It is not a bad idea to check your findings with someone whom you respect and trust to verify your

Table 11.4 Mega groups by worldwide gross income

				Gross income				
Rank				**Worldwide**			**U.S.**	
1988	**1987**	**Group**	**1988**	**1987**	**% chg**	**1988**	**1987**	**% chg**
1	1	Saatchi & Saatchi PLC	$1,990	$1,685	18.2	$921	$823	12.0
2	2	Interpublic Group of Cos.	1,260	993	26.9	464	390	18.9
3	4	WPP Group PLC	1,173	893	31.5	638	492	29.8
4	3	Omnicom Group	986	896	10.6	585	549	6.5
5	5	Ogilvy Group	865	759	14.0	393	366	7.4
6	6	Eurocom	500	420	19.0	27	25	9.3
7	7	WCRS Group	335	240	39.3	100	89	12.4
8	8	Lowe Howard-Spink & Bell	197	149	32.8	58	57	1.3
9	11	Bozell Inc.	194	NA	NA	165	NA	NA
10	10	GGK Holding AG	85	52	62.6	25	10	136.1
11	9	Lopex PLC*	68	54	26.4	10	8	14.3

Notes: Dollars are in millions. Only a group's percentage of ownership of agencies is included in its total. *Figures represent only advertising business, Alliance International. Source: *Advertising Age.*

decisions. You must take into account how your own strengths and weaknesses relate to the advertising field. Consider the types of employment available within an agency or a corporate department and decide where, if anywhere, you will fit. Success in advertising takes a particular type of personality and temperament. You should make sure that you possess the personal characteristics necessary for success in this field.

Next, you should find out where you are likely to find the kind of job you want. Then make your plans to cover that territory. If you want to work for a big agency, concentrate in the major advertising centers like New York City, Chicago, Detroit, Dallas, Boston, San Francisco, Minneapolis, or Los Angeles. If you think a smaller agency may be your first

Table 11.5 Mega groups minus non-media advertising

				Worldwide gross income	
Rank					
1988	**1987**	**Group**	**1988**	**1987**	**% chg**
1	1	Saatchi & Saatchi PLC	$1,474	$1,335	10.5
2	2	Interpublic Group of Cos.	1,260	993	26.9
3	3	Omnicom Group	963	872	10.4
4	4	Ogilvy Group	715	633	13.0
5	5	WPP Group PLC	613	520	17.7
6	6	Eurocom	500	420	19.0
7	7	WCRS Group	254	216	17.6
8	8	Lowe Howard-Spink & Bell	175	135	29.1
9	9	Bozell Inc.	173	NA	NA
10	9	GGK Holding AG	85	59	43.4
11	10	Lopex PLC (Alliance Int'l)	68	54	26.4

Note: Dollars are in millions. Source: *Advertising Age.*

Table 11.6 SAATCHI & SAATCHI CO. PLC

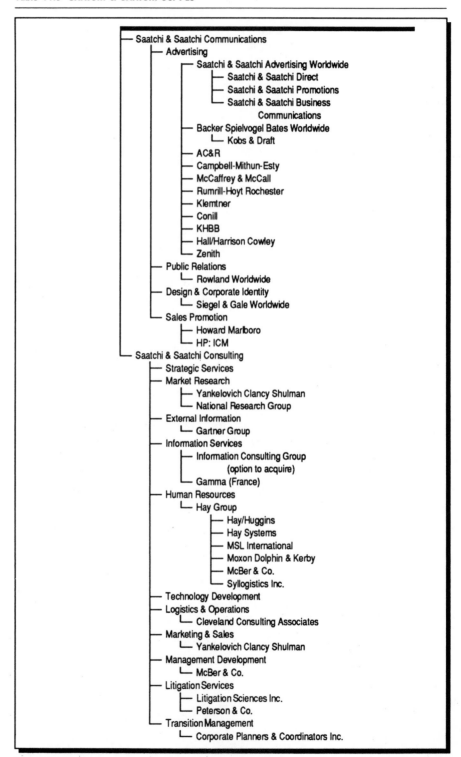

Saatchi & Saatchi Communications
- Advertising
  - Saatchi & Saatchi Advertising Worldwide
    - Saatchi & Saatchi Direct
    - Saatchi & Saatchi Promotions
    - Saatchi & Saatchi Business Communications
  - Backer Spielvogel Bates Worldwide
    - Kobs & Draft
  - AC&R
  - Campbell-Mithun-Esty
  - McCaffrey & McCall
  - Rumrill-Hoyt Rochester
  - Klemtner
  - Conill
  - KHBB
  - Hall/Harrison Cowley
  - Zenith
- Public Relations
  - Rowland Worldwide
- Design & Corporate Identity
  - Siegel & Gale Worldwide
- Sales Promotion
  - Howard Marlboro
  - HP: ICM

Saatchi & Saatchi Consulting
- Strategic Services
- Market Research
  - Yankelovich Clancy Shulman
  - National Research Group
- External Information
  - Gartner Group
- Information Services
  - Information Consulting Group (option to acquire)
  - Gamma (France)
- Human Resources
  - Hay Group
    - Hay/Huggins
    - Hay Systems
    - MSL International
    - Moxon Dolphin & Kerby
    - McBer & Co.
    - Syllogistics Inc.
- Technology Development
- Logistics & Operations
  - Cleveland Consulting Associates
- Marketing & Sales
  - Yankelovich Clancy Shulman
- Management Development
  - McBer & Co.
- Litigation Services
  - Litigation Sciences Inc.
  - Peterson & Co.
- Transition Management
  - Corporate Planners & Coordinators Inc.

Source: *Advertising Age*

Table 11.7 Top 25 U.S. cities by local shop billings

		Total local shop billings			Reported
Rank	City	1988	1987	% chg	shops
1	New York	$21,068	$19,202	9.7	169
2	Chicago	5,941	5,292	12.3	80
3	Los Angeles	3,308	2,924	13.1	57
4	Detroit	3,093	2,620	18.1	31
5	San Francisco	1,467	1,456	0.8	34
6	Boston	1,058	972	8.8	25
7	Minneapolis	993	917	8.3	20
8	Dallas	932	850	9.6	16
9	Philadelphia	804	771	4.2	26
10	Cleveland	643	615	4.5	16
11	Atlanta	620	560	10.6	24
12	St. Louis	581	531	9.5	9
13	Houston	401	379	5.8	14
14	Pittsburgh	321	310	3.5	7
15	Baltimore	314	291	7.8	8
16	Washington	310	283	9.6	8
17	Milwaukee	290	263	10.3	13
18	Seattle	248	225	10.2	10
19	Kansas City, Mo.	241	225	7.1	10
20	Rochester, N.Y.	228	219	4.2	9
21	Stamford, Conn.	218	204	7.1	12
22	Richmond, Va.	175	151	16.2	5
23	Columbus, Ohio	152	132	14.8	5
24	Miami	130	110	18.2	12
25	Raleigh, N.C.	129	122	5.1	2

Notes: Dollars are in millions. Source: *Advertising Age*

choice, you can look in these same cities as well as smaller cities and perhaps in your own home town. Table 11.7 shows the top twenty-five advertising cities by local shop billings.

The *Standard Directory of Advertising Agencies* will give you locations and sizes of different firms. You should be able to find a copy at your local library or try to borrow one from a friend in advertising. Reading trade publications such as *Advertising Age* to look at the help-wanted ads and see which agencies landed new accounts may provide you with direction as to which agencies are looking for new employees.

RÉSUMÉS

After you have pinpointed the type of job you want and where you would like to work, you must prepare a résumé outlining your qualifications. Most people approach this task with considerable apprehension, no matter how far along they are in their careers. The challenge of writing a résumé is to say enough to arouse interest and convey assurance that you are truly a qualified applicant, without overstating your accomplishments and abilities in a way that is likely to turn off your potential employer. Remember, advertising is communication and selling. Here is your chance to show how well you can sell yourself. It will help if you follow these basic rules:

1. Be concise.
2. List relevant employment activities in reverse order (the most recent one first). Be sure you include part-time jobs you have had, especially those in sales or media that might be pertinent to advertising. Often these job experiences are more important than your academic achievements.
3. Try not to overstate or understate achievements. If you are modest, do not forget that the person looking at your résumé can only make a judgment on the basis of what is written. If you are inclined to be a little exuberant, remember that exaggerated claims are sure to reduce your credibility. Be as objective as possible.
4. Include academic achievements and especially extracurricular activities that show a flair for creativity and promotion. Perhaps you were chairperson for the senior ball or handled publicity for the school football team. These are important activities and should be mentioned. Be sure to include any evidence of leadership qualities (class officer, team captain), as these qualities are always in demand.
5. Record information about pertinent hobbies or leisure-time activities, like painting, photography, short-story writing, or music composition. These things are closely related to the work in advertising.
6. Do not forget to include your address and telephone number.
7. Give references that include the names, titles, and addresses of three or four people whose judgments and opinions about you are likely to carry some weight. If they happen to be people in advertising, so much the better.
8. Prepare your résumé on standard size 8½" × 11" white bond paper. It is easiest for people to handle.

The sample résumé on the next page should be helpful to you.

Of course, if you have had one or more full-time jobs, you should name them, saying what you did, what your responsibilities were, and citing any bona fide accomplishments. Additionally, if you were part of a team that did something noteworthy, mention it. However, be sure to give the credit to the team effort and do not claim that you did it all by yourself. Personnel people are very skeptical of such claims and are likely to consider them, and the person who makes them, as transparently exaggerated. It is not worth the risk.

Donald L. Van Dyke
1444 S. Maple Avenue
Springfield, IL 60153
Phone: (302) 555-0790

Employment Sought

Account Executive Trainee

Educational Background

College: University of Illinois, B.A. in English, 1989
Minor: Advertising
Honors and Activities: honors graduate, college radio station (4 years; 1 year as business manager), debate team, drama club president.

High School: Tecumseh Senior High School, Peoria, IL Graduated June 1985
Honors and Activities: school newspaper (assistant editor and official photographer).

Employment Experience (Summer Employment Only)

1983
Strongin Research Company
443 Wickham Way
Peoria, IL 61611
Ms. Barbara A. Guden

1982
Don's Car Wash
324 Broadway
Peoria, IL 61642
Mr. Donald Rolfe

References

Mr. Warren F. Flint, Jr.
Vice-President
Mutual National Bank
Springfield, IL 60153

Mr. David G. Ruesch
Hufford, Turner & Stern
1657 W. Main Street
Peoria, IL 61604

To accompany your résumé, it is a good idea to write a letter setting forth the job you want and adding some detail as to why you believe you are qualified. Do not, however, discuss salary. Such discussions come after you and your future employer have agreed that there is a mutually acceptable opening for you.

If you have letters of recommendation (or of commendation), either attach copies to your résumés or make them part of your portfolio. The more evidence you have of your employability, the better.

Never hesitate to ask personal and family friends or former employers to provide you with introductions to anyone who might have a job for you. They probably will be happy to assist you, and the contact they provide will help you broaden your network of associations in the business.

PORTFOLIOS

In addition to a résumé, you should also prepare a portfolio of your best advertising work before you set your interviews. Here again, you probably face the problem of not having many published samples of your work. Do, however, include articles you have written for the student paper and relevant projects you prepared for class. But do not include any sample unless you feel it represents your best work. If you don't have many samples, create some.

The thing most likely to attract an employer is your creativity. How good are you at coming up with original, sparkling ideas? In creating ads for your portfolio, you need to demonstrate these qualities.

Study familiar products and try to come up with a novel way to sell them. Do some research on the product to determine its present, and possibly unknown, uses. Study what benefits the product has for you and other consumers. Just as you would for a real advertising campaign, base your ad on what you learn.

What you include in your ad also depends on what type of job you are seeking. If you want a position as an artist, the design of the ad should be of primary importance. This does not mean that you need to do a finished ad—just enough to show your capabilities. And don't fail to include at least a headline for your ad.

On the other hand, if you see yourself mainly as a writer, the design for the ad does not have to be detailed, although clearly indicate the illustration area within the ad. Concentrate on writing a striking headline (or more than one) as well as at least part of the body copy, the explanatory copy for the ad. In both cases, if you have any knowledge or experience in doing television production, scripts and storyboards showing the major frames in your ad can also be included in your portfolio. An excellent book to use as reference in preparing your portfolio is *How to Put Your Book Together and Get a Job in Advertising* by Maxine Paetro, who worked as creative manager for Foote, Cone & Belding.

INTERVIEWS

Once you have prepared your résumé and portfolio, you are ready to go on your first interview. Try to get an appointment with the agency's creative director, copy chief, or the head of any other department that interests you. Personnel people are not as likely to be interested or impressed with your work as department heads. When the time for the interview arrives, be punctual. Remember, good manners and proper dress are recognized quickly, and first impressions are important, especially in a business like advertising that emphasizes "image."

Interviews can be nerve-racking experiences because you will probably be expected to do most of the talking. The line between "running off at the mouth" and not saying enough can be a very thin one, particularly if you encounter an interviewer who stares at you silently. Consequently, you should consider what you want to communicate and carefully organize what you are going to say. Your emphasis should be on why you want a job *with this company* (not why you want a job; the interviewer knows that) and why you believe you are qualified for the position.

Go prepared with intelligent questions about the kind of work available and the contribution you can make. Do research about the prospective employer before the interview. Listen to the answers and try to create a dialogue. Ask questions that encourage the interviewer to talk with you. The interviewer will like you better if you can get him or her to do some of the talking. Whatever you do, *do not* focus your questions on such things as vacation policies, employee benefits, or anything else that suggests that you are more interested in what the company can do for you than in what you can do for the company. The employer will provide this information, usually near the end of the interview. If it is not offered, the appropriate time to discuss it is *after* the employer has had an opportunity to bring up the subject. Before leaving, determine when you might learn the outcome of your interview. Ask if you may phone back in two or three days. Make an effort to keep the door open for future contact. If employment seems unlikely, ask the interviewer if he or she knows of an opportunity at another company. You may pick up a good lead that will help you land your first job.

Unfortunately, few job applicants are hired at the first place they visit, and trying to get on someone's payroll often is time-consuming and discouraging. For those reasons, neither let your initial hopes run too high nor your early disappointments run too deep. Getting the right job, like most other worthwhile achievements in life, requires a systematic approach, hard work, determination, and persistence.

ON-THE-JOB TRAINING

Training in Entry-Level Positions

It used to be customary for a beginner to start in either print production or traffic. Some agencies still start newcomers in these departments, but the length of time they stay there is usually brief.

Today, it is more common to place beginners in other departments such as media, research, or in a training program that systematically moves them from place to place. In this manner, it is certain they will have an opportunity to become familiar with the various agency activities before being given definitive job assignments. Training programs differ from agency to agency in the sequence of departments that are observed, the length of time devoted to each, and in the amount of actual participation as opposed to observation.

Bearing in mind that these differences do exist, a typical course of instruction might include the following:

Traffic and Print Production

1. Agency procedures.
2. Assignments.
3. Relationship with other departments.
4. Printing processes, tours of printing and engraving plants and typesetting shops.
5. Planning and buying print material other than advertisements—booklets, brochures, posters, displays.
6. Legal requirements.
7. Security regulations and procedures.
8. Correspondence, mailing, and shipping.

Research Department

1. Gathering and analyzing market information.
2. Developing a marketing or advertising strategy.
3. Designing market research procedures and questionnaires.
4. Using and reporting results.
5. Using copy research in its various forms for print and broadcast.
6. Identifying and evaluating competitive media research.
7. Measuring the reach (number of people who see or hear the advertising) and frequency (how often they see or hear it) of various media choices and selecting from various media alternatives.

Media Services Department

1. Fitting the media plan and strategy to marketing and advertising goals.
2. Evaluating and contracting for network programs and spots.
3. Evaluating and buying market-by-market programs and spots.
4. Evaluating and selecting magazines and newspapers that best fit each advertising plan.

Creative Services Department

1. Understanding how advertising is designed to fit the specifications of the plan and what thinking and discussion go into developing the plan.
2. Learning how illustrative material is chosen and sources from which it may be obtained.
3. Understanding how a TV commercial takes its form, from rough idea, to storyboard, to finished product, including visits to film studios, animation studios, and on-location filming.
4. Learning how a radio commercial comes into being and different techniques available, and visiting recording studios.
5. Casting and talent selection.
6. Codes and rules of the involved guilds.
7. Legal and regulatory restrictions and guidelines.
8. Budget control.

Account Services Department

1. Duties and assignments.
2. Formulating a marketing strategy.
3. Fitting the advertising plan to marketing strategy.
4. Reporting results of client meetings, including assignments for action.
5. Dealing with agency personnel in other departments.
6. Managing the client's advertising budget.
7. Directing agency activities for a profit.
8. Legal and regulatory consideration.

If the agency is engaged in promotional or merchandising activities, there may also be some instruction in these areas. It would probably include these topics:

1. Special requirements of sales promotion copy.
2. Sales promotion art and design.
3. Organizing sales meetings, including presentation techniques.
4. Using premiums, giveaways, and contests, and selecting suppliers.
5. Finding and taking advantage of publicity opportunities.
6. Legal and regulatory requirements; important because each state has different rules with respect to contests and premium offers.
7. Managing the budget.

It is clear that there are different theories about how best to train beginners and to help them to learn all the facets of the job. The important thing to remember, however, is that whatever procedure is used, it will be only as effective and valuable as each trainee's interest and application permit it to be. If the desire to learn the advertising business is strong, it really does not matter how the training program is designed. In addition, it should be remembered that such programs are only the beginning. For the true advertising professional, the learning process never stops.

Large mass-marketers of consumer goods (particularly in the food field), such as Procter & Gamble, General Mills, Kellogg, and others, offer excellent training programs in advertising. There is a definite advantage to such programs in that one learns of the movement of goods from the client's point of view. This experience, gained early on, can be useful in later work in an advertising agency. By training within the corporate advertising department, one can learn about the effects of an advertising campaign on the movement and profitability of goods over a period of time. Of course, this experience does not have to lead to agency work; there are plenty of lifetime opportunities in advertising in the corporate setting.

ADVANCEMENT

After working on the job for a while, you will no doubt start thinking about promotion and advancement. Here again, it is impossible to set down any definite guidelines. Advertising is not like the federal Civil Service in which so many years at one job level entitle an employee to move up to the next higher spot. How fast you progress in advertising depends almost entirely on your performance, ability to acquire the necessary skills, maturity, grasp of the business, and the success of your employer, whether it is an advertising agency or corporate marketer. It is impossible to make an absolute statement about how quickly and to what level a new employee will advance in the advertising business; however, here are some general observations which apply to most beginners.

Do not expect to begin your advancement immediately. If you are hired right out of college as a trainee, it will probably be a year or two before you find yourself working full-time at some specialty—account work, media research, creative work, or whatever. From that point on, your progress can be rapid, if you are capable and if there are not a number of equally competent people ahead of you.

A résumé for Mary B. Powers might look something like the one on the next page after a few years of employment.

Let us assume that you have a clear track, that the agency you are working for is successful and growing, and that you have the necessary

Mary B. Powers
144 W. Diversey Parkway
Chicago, IL 60657
Phone: (312) 555-9080

Employment Sought

Assistant Account Executive

Employment Experience

1989 Assistant Copywriter
Fiddle & Ross Advertising
1000 N. Michigan Avenue
Chicago, IL 60601
Mr. Leonard I. Fiddle

Wrote body copy and headlines for Ajax detergent and Pepsi accounts.

1988 Media Researcher
Fiddle & Ross Advertising
1000 N. Michigan Avenue
Chicago, IL 60601
Ms. Kathleen M. Schultz

Worked for media buyer and evaluated media and markets for clients in the travel field.

Educational Background

College:	University of Illinois B.A. in English, 1986
Important Courses:	psychology, history, French, and Spanish.
Honors and Activities:	honors graduate, editor of student newspaper, debate team, sorority president.
High School:	Temple High School Robinson, IL Graduated June 1982
Honors and Activities:	school newspaper assistant editor and official photographer, drama club, swimming team captain.

References

Mr. Michael K. Urban
The Rogus Agency
1647 W. Main St.
Peoria, IL 61604

Mr. Raymond B. Walters
Schuldt, Psujek and Selden, Inc.
141 W. Pierce St.
Chicago, IL 60611

ability. In that case, it would be natural for your steps up the ladder to proceed at a fairly fast pace, possibly as follows:

- one and a half years training in media
- two years as an assistant account executive
- five years as account executive and senior account executive
- two to three years as account manager, becoming a vice-president
- three to five years as management supervisor, possibly becoming an executive vice-president, depending on the agency's structure
- agency president

At some point during your advancement, you will become a member of the agency's board of directors and perhaps a stockholder. And as you progress, you will have opportunities to acquire increasing amounts of stock in the agency. Exactly the same kind of progression takes place on the creative side of the business. It can also happen in media or research.

It used to be a rarity for a large and prestigious agency to have a president (or chief executive officer) who was not well into his or her forties; however, this is no longer the case, especially in advertising. So, if you are especially dynamic and talented, you can make it to the top in a relatively short period of time.

Is this opportunity for men only? By no means. One of the biggest and most successful agencies in the country, Wells, Rich, Greene, Inc., was started by a woman, Mary Wells Lawrence, and she was its only chief executive officer for many years. More and more women are sitting on agency boards of directors and holding top positions as advertising directors in large corporations. The trend in this direction is strong, but men still outnumber women in the most important posts. Though there is a high proportion of women in lower-level jobs, there are also many different types of opportunities for women at all levels.

It should be acknowledged at this point that most of the extremely successful women have risen to the top from early experience in the media, research, or creative sides of the business. So far, except for fields like fashion, cosmetics, food, and other areas of traditional feminine interest, not many women have held high-level jobs in account management. It is altogether unclear why this should be, but as of this writing, it is a fact. It will change as time passes, if enough capable women are interested in careers in advertising.

If you are member of a minority group and have the necessary talent, advertising offers real opportunities for you. Every sizable company or agency is eager to add people of different ethnic backgrounds to its staff. In most advertising centers, minorities are in great demand and also in short supply. And as a growing number of agencies recognize the potential of marketing to ethnic groups as special markets, these opportunities will increase.

There are also black and Hispanic advertising agencies, generally concentrated in major urban areas. They usually specialize in advertising to the black or Spanish-speaking markets and solicit clients to reach these sectors only. These agencies have grown tremendously in the last decade and offer many opportunities.

FREE-LANCING OR STARTING YOUR OWN AGENCY

Nearly everyone gets started in advertising working for someone else, whether that someone is an advertising agency, a corporate advertising department, or a firm specializing in some aspect of advertising. Before you should consider free-lancing—that is, selling your creative or marketing skills as an individual to various advertisers and advertising agencies—or starting an agency of your own, you need to gain experience and enough skill to make yourself marketable to prospective clients.

Free-lancing provides a good first step in self-employment, especially for people in the creative side of advertising. As a free-lance artist or copywriter, you will probably work on a project-by-project basis for either an advertising agency or for the advertiser.

You will very likely do many of the same things that you would do if you were working for the client or agency.

Successful free-lancing hinges on understanding and executing with speed whatever is needed. There is no employer to train you. If you want to free-lance, you must know your business. Of course, unlike a steady job with an advertiser or agency, you will have to find the work yourself. You cannot wait until someone calls. The skill with which you make and expand your job contacts will be the deciding factor in how successful you are at free-lancing. Join a professional organization and keep track of former colleagues and friends who know your capabilities and understand your talent.

Free-lancing or starting your own agency has many advantages. If you are good and develop a reputation with a following, you have the potential to earn more than an employee. Of course, unlike a steady job, you can't always count on a paycheck coming in once or twice a month. There are many peaks and valleys, and you need the financial resources and steady emotions to carry you through the low periods. Sometimes there will be no work and sometimes people will take a long time to pay, so you must have financial reserves to carry you through the slow times. You also have the satisfaction and flexibility of being your own boss. On the other hand, you may find yourself working harder than ever. This will undoubtedly be true during the first years when you are attempting to establish yourself. Since you will probably have to pay the media, suppliers, and operating expenses long before you have received payment from your clients, it is essential that you have enough cash reserves (at least six months of estimated operating expenses is a must to set up shop). Also, since it takes time to get clients and develop a reasonable flow of steady business and since some clients will take up to four or five months to pay their bills, you would be wise to have a resource to turn to if further capital is needed. Do not forget that you have to eat and pay your staff as well. So by all means, take the plunge, if you have the experience and think the time is right. But before you jump, test the water.

Once an agency has been in business for a while, its owners may want to become members of the American Association of Advertising Agencies (AAAA). Gaining membership in this organization is a good bit harder than getting started in the business. The agency must be able to demonstrate its financial stability, must be prepared to adhere to the AAAA's code of practice, must be nominated by some other agency, must be approved by other members, and must be able to secure references from a number of media with which it has done business. In short, it must be recognized as responsible, established, and professional.

If you decide that starting your own agency would be a great idea, be sure that you consult a lawyer, get the support of a banker, and establish satisfactory credit. It is too important and risky a step to take without proper planning. Still, it could be the most rewarding and satisfying step you ever take in the course of establishing your career in advertising.

OPPORTUNITIES IN SMALLER AGENCIES

Your first thought when beginning to look for a job in advertising will probably be, "How can I get a job at a large, big-city agency?" Before focusing your job search at the larger agencies, be sure to take a look at the unique opportunities at a smaller agency, or even a small-town agency.

There are many agencies across the country that offer a different, but no less challenging, work environment than the larger agencies. These smaller agencies may be found in the major advertising cities, or in smaller cities and towns across the country. What you will find in a smaller agency that you won't find in a larger agency is a less structured work environment and a broader spectrum of diversified work. With less staff, a small agency offers one the opportunity to learn and master many facets of the advertising business that you are unlikely to experience at a large agency. Remember, though, that just because an agency is small does not mean that it lacks a top-notch staff with big-agency talent. Working at a small agency may mean a step down in size, but not necessarily in the quality of the work. As there are advantages and disadvantages to working in a large firm, so there are advantages and disadvantages in working in a smaller firm.

Nevertheless, the competition for jobs in this environment is just as fierce as the competition for jobs in a larger agency. A good idea when looking for a job at a small agency is to take a look at the agency's client list. Find an agency that has a good variety of clients because a diversified pool of clients means a fuller working experience for you. Client lists can be found in *The Agency Red Book,* which you will find in most libraries and in most agencies. With larger agencies, generally the client list is wide and diversified. With the right search, you stand a better chance to find the job of your choice.

SALARIES

Finally, let's take a look at the chart that follows, which shows the salary levels in the advertising industry for 1989. This table (11.8) is divided also by agency billings size. Remember that these figures are merely averages

Table 11.8 Average total compensation* by position—1989 (By agency billings size.)

	Up to $5 million	$5–10 million	$10–25 million	$25–100 million	Over $100 million
CEO (Independent)	$81,800	$140,600	$162,700	$240,800	$438,500
CEO (Subsidiary)	84,000[1]	75,300[1]	75,300	123,600	249,900
President/COO	78,100	91,600	125,800	241,100	270,900
Branch office manager	42,400	48,200	62,000	121,300	169,800
Executive vice president	60,200	86,500	94,800	136,700	194,800
Chief financial officer	33,600	57,600	70,800	95,100	175,600
Controller	26,300	36,500	37,800	47,400	74,600
Data processing manager	21,200	21,100	32,600	37,800	58,300
Human resources director	37,400[1]	18,100[1]	30,300	51,500	70,100
Traffic manager	20,300	22,600	24,900	26,100	34,600
Creative director	51,200	70,800	80,700	121,800	180,900
Associate creative director	33,500	56,600	64,300	78,700	106,900
Creative supervisor	34,300	31,900[1]	51,500[1]	57,700	80,800
Senior art director	36,100	43,900	39,200	54,900	77,500
Art director	25,500	29,000	29,900	37,100	45,600
Senior copywriter	34,000	37,600	36,300	51,000	67,600
Copywriter	31,400	27,000	34,600	37,700	46,700
Junior copywriter	20,100	25,900	24,600	30,300	31,400
Media director	29,600	40,600	45,800	61,600	92,200
Associate media director	20,800	24,300	26,400	39,500	61,800
Broadcast production manager	27,000[1]	26,800	39,200	39,400	89,700
Producer	30,300	20,900[1]	31,100	42,700	63,300
Print production manager	27,000	32,500	33,900	45,500	50,900
Public relations manager	35,100	40,500	49,900	54,400	75,600
Business development manager	43,600	47,900	62,200	126,900	133,700
Market research manager	24,000	69,900[1]	50,700	64,000	78,100
Director account management	54,000	59,100	79,200	97,800	120,300
Account planning manager	43,300	54,000	57,600	62,000	70,000
Senior account executive	41,500	42,900	45,800	62,700	51,900
Account executive	30,100	31,500	29,100	35,300	36,100

*Salary and bonuses. [1]Limited sample. Source: © 1989 by Cole Surveys. Reprinted from *Advertising Age.*

Table 11.9 Highest total cash compensation by position/1989

CEO (subsidiary)	$1,051,200
Creative director	820,500
CEO (independent)	750,000
President	677,000
Branch office manager	546,800
Chief financial officer	459,500
Executive vice president	350,800
Director account management	310,000
Associate creative director	265,000
Business development manager	257,100
Broadcast production manager	225,000
Creative supervisor	187,500
Senior account executive	184,800
Media director	163,500
Human resources director	160,000
Senior copywriter	157,500
Account planning manager	155,000
Controller	150,600
Senior art director	150,000
Market research manager	145,000
Producer	135,000
Associate media director	120,000
Public relations manager	117,000
Data processing manager	102,000
Art director	100,000
Copywriter	94,500
Print production manager	93,000
Account executive	80,000
Junior copywriter	73,000
Traffic manager	66,000

© 1989 by Cole Surveys. Reprinted from *Advertising Age*.

and that you will find that salaries do, of course, vary from agency to agency.

Table 11.9 shows the absolute highest salaries for various positions. This will give you an idea of what might happen if you become a superstar, though salaries this high generally come after years of hard work and success in the field of advertising.

Okay, now you've had your briefing on the advertising business. The rest is up to you. If you are in the midst of finishing your education, then apply yourself and learn as much as possible. If you're in the job market now, either for an entry-level position or anxious to further your career, plunge ahead and accept the challenge with enthusiasm. I wish you good luck! I am sure that you will find your career in advertsing to be challenging, exciting, and rewarding.

APPENDIX A: RECOMMENDED READING

CAREER GUIDANCE

Career Publishing Corporation. *Advertising Career Directory*. New York, NY.

National Association of Broadcasters. *Careers in Television*. Washington, DC.

Greenberg, Jan. *Advertising Careers*. New York, NY: H. Holt, 1987

Laskin, David. *Getting Into Advertising*. New York, NY: Ballantine, 1986

Noronha, Shonan. *Careers in Communications*. Lincolnwood, IL: VGM Career Horizons, 1987.

Paetro, Maxine. *How to Put Your Book Together and Get a Job in Advertising*. New York, NY: Dutton, 1980

Pattis, S. William. *Opportunities in Advertising Careers*. Lincolnwood, IL: VGM Career Horizons, 1988

Pattis, S. William. *Opportunities in Magazine Publishing Careers*. Lincolnwood, IL: VGM Career Horizons, 1988.

Rotman, Morris B. *Opportunities in Public Relations Careers*. Lincolnwood, IL: VGM Career Horizons, 1988.

Steinberg, Margery. *Opportunities in Marketing Careers*. Lincolnwood, IL: VGM Career Horizons, 1988.

White, Roderick. *Advertising: What It Is and How To Do It*. New York, NY: McGraw-Hill Book Company, 1981.

THEORY AND PRACTICE

Book, Albert C., and C. Dennis Schick. *Fundamentals of Copy and Layout.* Lincolnwood, IL: NTC Business Books, 1985.

Bouvee, Courtland L., and William F. Arens. *Contemporary Advertising.* 2d ed. Homewood, IL: Richard D. Irwin, Inc., 1986.

Center, Allen H., and Scott H. Cutlip. *Effective Public Relations.* 5th ed. Englewood Cliffs, NJ: Prentice-Hall, Inc., 1978.

Favre, Jean-Paul, and Andre November. *Color and Communication.* New York, NY: Hastings House, 1979.

Fletcher, Winston. *Teach Yourself Advertising.* New York, NY: McKay, 1978.

Gardner, Herbert S., Jr. *The Advertising Agency Business.* 2d ed. Lincolnwood, IL: NTC Business Books, 1988.

Garfunkel, Stanley. *Developing the Advertising Plan: A Practical Guide.* New York, NY: Random House, 1980.

Gibson, Arthur, et al. *Truth in Advertising.* Lewiston, NY: Edwin Mellen Press, 1982.

Gilson, Christopher and Harold W. Berkman. *Advertising: Concepts and Strategies.* 2d ed. New York, NY: Random House, 1987.

Hollike, Bert. *How To Be Your Own Advertising Agency.* New York, NY: McGraw-Hill, 1981.

Norris, James S. *Advertising.* Reston, VA: Reston, 1980.

Rothschild, Michael L. *Advertising: From Fundamentals to Strategies.* Lexington, MA: D.C. Heath and Company, 1987.

Schultz, Don E. *Essentials of Advertising Strategy.* 2d ed. Lincolnwood, IL: NTC Business books, 1988.

Schultz, Don E., Dennis G. Martin, and William P. Brown. *Strategic Advertising Campaigns.* 2d ed. Lincolnwood, IL: NTC Business Books, 1984.

Sroge, Maxwell. *How to Create Successful Catalogs.* Lincolnwood, IL: NTC Business Books, 1985.

Stone, Bob. *Successful Direct Marketing Methods.* 3d ed. Lincolnwood, IL: NTC Business Books, 1984.

Urdang, Laurence, ed. *Dictionary of Advertising.* Lincolnwood, IL: NTC Business Books, 1986.

White, Hooper. *How to Produce Effective TV Commercials.* 2d ed. Lincolnwood, IL: NTC Business Books, 1986.

DIRECTORIES

Ayer Directory of Publications
N.W. Ayer ABH International
West Washington Square
Philadelphia, PA 19106

Broadcasting Yearbook
Broadcasting Publications, Inc.
1735 DeSales Street NW
Washington, DC 20036

Standard Directory of Advertising Agencies
3004 Glenview Road
Wilmette, IL 60091

Standard Directory of Advertisers
3004 Glenview Road
Wilmette, IL 60091

Standard Rate and Data Service
3004 Glenview Road
Wilmette, IL 60091

Working Press of the Nation, Vol. 5
The National Research Bureau
Burlington, VA 26710

PERIODICALS

A&SP Newsline, Chicago, IL.

Ad Media, Ad-Media Enterprises, Columbia, MD.

Advertising Age, Crain Communications, Inc., Chicago, IL.

Adweek, A/S/M Communications, New York, NY.

The Bach Letter, Henry Bach Association, Inc., New York, NY.

Briefings, Advertising Specialty Institute, Trevose, PA.

Business Marketing, Crain Communications, Inc., Chicago, IL.

Career Forum, Women in Communications, Inc., New York, NY.

Creative, Magazines/Creative, Inc., New York, NY.

Dartnell Sales and Marketing Service, Dartnell Corp., Chicago, IL.

Direct Marketing Magazine, Hanson Publishing Group, Garden City, NY.

D.M. News, Mill Hollow Corp., 19 West Twenty-first Street, New York, NY 10010.

Folio, Hanson Publishing Group, Stamford, CT.

Graphic Arts Buyer, A.D.A. Publishing Co., New York, NY.

Inside Media, Hanson Publishing Group, Stamford, CT.

IPRA Review, Journal of the International Public Relations Association, Pergamon Press Ltd., Elmsford, NY.

Journal of Advertising Research, Advertising Research Foundation, New York, NY.

Modern Publicity, The Viking Press, New York, NY.

PR Reporter, PR Publications Co., Inc., Exeter, NH.

Public Relations Journal, Public Relations Society of America, New York, NY.

Publicist, Public Relations Aids, Inc., New York, NY.

Sales and Marketing Management, Bill Communications, New York, NY.

Television/Radio Age, Television Editorial Corp., New York, NY.

Viewpoints: The Journal for Data Collection, Marketing Research Association, Chicago, IL.

APPENDIX B: NATIONAL GROUPS AND ASSOCIATIONS

The Advertising Club of New
 York
155 East Fifty-fifth Street, Suite
 202
New York, NY 10022

Ad II Club of New York
285 Madison Avenue
New York, NY 10017

The Advertising Council
825 Third Avenue
New York, NY 10022

Advertising Research Foundation
3 East Fifty-fourth Street
New York, NY 10019

Advertising Women of New York
153 East Fifty-seventh Street
New York, NY 10017

American Advertising Federation
1225 Connecticut Avenue
Washington, DC 20036

American Association of
 Advertising Agencies
666 Third Avenue
New York, NY 10021

American Institute of Graphic
 Arts
1059 Third Avenue
New York, NY 10021

American Marketing Association
250 South Wacker Drive, Suite
 2000
Chicago, IL 60600

Art Directors Club of New York
1488 Madison Avenue
New York, NY 10022

Association of National
 Advertisers
155 East Forty-fourth Street
New York, NY 10017

Business/Professional Advertising
 Association
205 East Forty-second Street
New York, NY 10017

Council of Better Business
 Bureaus
1515 Wilson Boulevard
Arlington, VA 22209

Council of Sales Promotion
 Agencies
1831 Chestnut Street
Philadelphia, PA 19103

Direct Marketing Association
6 East Forty-third Street
New York, NY 10017

Foundation for Public Relations
 Research and Education
845 Third Avenue
New York, NY 10022

International Advertising
 Association
475 Fifth Avenue
New York, NY 10017

International Federation of
 Advertising Agencies
Sarasota Bank Building
Sarasota, FL 33577

Magazine Publishers Association
575 Lexington Avenue
New York, NY 10017

National Advertising Review
 Board
845 Third Avenue
New York, NY 10022

National Association of
 Broadcasters
1771 N Street NW
Washington, DC 20036

Newspaper Advertising Bureau
485 Lexington Avenue
New York, NY 10017

National Association of Publisher
 Representatives
114 East Thirty-second Street,
 Suite 1406
New York, NY 10016

The One Club
3 West Eighteenth Street, Third
 Floor
New York, NY 10011

Outdoor Advertising Association
 of America
1899 L Street NW, Suite 403
Washington, DC 20036

Point of Purchase Advertising
 Institute
60 East Forty-second Street
New York, NY 10017

Premium Advertising Association
 of America
420 Lexington Avenue
New York, NY 10017

Print Advertising Association
10-64 Jackson Avenue
Long Island City, NY 11101

Promotional Marketing
 Association of America
420 Lexington Avenue
New York, NY 10017

Public Relations Society of
    America
845 Third Avenue
New York, NY 10022

Radio Advertising Bureau
485 Lexington Avenue
New York, NY 10017

Retail Advertising Association
67 East Oak Street
Chicago, IL 60611

The Society of Illustrators
128 East Sixty-third Street
New York, NY 10021

Specialty Advertising Association
    International
1404 Walnut Hill Land
Irving, TX 75062

Specialty Advertising Information
    Bureau
740 North Rush Street
Chicago, IL 60611

Television Bureau of Advertising
485 Lexington Avenue
New York, NY 10017

Television Information Office
745 Fifth Avenue
New York, NY 10022

The Transit Advertising
    Association, Inc.
60 East Forty-second Street, Suite
    1027
New York, NY 10165

APPENDIX C: COLLEGE ADVERTISING PROGRAMS

A selected list of colleges offering programs in advertising is presented below. Every effort has been made to make this a comprehensive list, but as changes can occur rapidly, you should also check with local and state schools and with the American Advertising Federation for any additional choices at the time you wish to choose a school.

In addition to colleges offering advertising programs, many other schools have courses in marketing, journalism, design, and other advertising-related courses which you will also want to investigate.

Alabama
University of Alabama
Tuscaloosa 35487

Arizona
Arizona State University
Tempe 85287

Northern Arizona University
Flagstaff 86001

Arkansas
University of Arkansas/Little Rock
Little Rock 72204

California
California State University/Fresno
Fresno 93740

California State University/Fullerton
Fullerton 92634

San Jose State University
San Jose 95192

Colorado
University of Colorado
Boulder 80309

Connecticut
University of Bridgeport
Bridgeport 06602

Florida
University of Central Florida
Orlando 32816

University of Florida
Gainesville 32611

Florida State University
Tallahassee 32306

University of South Florida
Tampa 33620

Georgia
University of Georgia
Athens 30602

Illinois
Columbia College
Chicago 60605

DePaul University
Chicago 60604

Northern Illinois University
DeKalb 60115

Northwestern University
Evanston 60201

Roosevelt University
Chicago 60605

Southern Illinois University
Carbondale 62901

University of Illinois
Urbana 61801

Indiana
Ball State University
Muncie 47306

Indiana University
Bloomington 47401

Iowa
Drake University
Des Moines 50311

Iowa State University
Ames 50011

Kansas
Kansas State University
Manhattan 66505

University of Kansas
Lawrence 66045

Wichita State University
Wichita 67208

Kentucky
Murray State University
Murray 42071

University of Kentucky
Lexington 40506

Western Kentucky University
Bowling Green 42101

Louisiana
Louisiana State University
Baton Rouge 70803

Maine
University of Maine
Orono 04473

Maryland
University of Maryland
College Park 20742

Massachusetts
Boston University
Boston 02215

Michigan
Ferris State College
Big Rapids 49307

Michigan State University
East Lansing 48824

Western Michigan University
Kalamazoo 49001

Minnesota
Moorehead State University
Moorehead 56560

University of Minnesota
Minneapolis 55455

Mississippi
University of Mississippi
University 38677

University of Southern Mississippi
Hattiesburg 39401

Missouri
University of Missouri
Columbia 65205

Nebraska
Creighton University
Omaha 68178

University of Nebraska
Lincoln 68588

Nevada
University of Nevada—Reno
Reno 89557

New Mexico
New Mexico State University
Las Cruces 88003

New York
City University of New York
New York 10010

College of New Rochelle
New Rochelle 10801

New York University
New York 10012

Syracuse University
Syracuse 13210

North Carolina
University of North Carolina
Chapel Hill 27514

North Dakota
University of North Dakota
Grand Forks 58202

Ohio
Bowling Green State University
Bowling Green 43403

Kent State University
Kent 44242

Ohio University
Athens 47501

University of Dayton
Dayton 45469

Youngstown State University
Youngstown 44555

Oklahoma
Central State University
Edmond 73034

Oklahoma State University
Stillwater 74078

University of Oklahoma
Norman 73019

Oregon
University of Oregon
Eugene 97403

Pennsylvania
Pennsylvania State University
University Park 16802

Temple University
Philadelphia 19122

Rhode Island
University of Rhode Island
Kingston 02881

South Carolina
University of South Carolina
Columbia 29208

South Dakota
South Dakota State University
Brookings 57007

Tennessee
Memphis State University
Memphis 38152

Middle Tennessee State University
Murphreysboro 37130

University of Tennessee
Knoxville 37916

Texas
North Texas State University
Denton 76203

Southern Methodist University
Dallas 75275

Southwest Texas State University
San Marcos 78666

Texas Christian University
Fort Worth 76129

Texas Tech University
Lubbock 79409

University of Texas at Austin
Austin 78712

Utah
Brigham Young University
Provo 84602

Virginia
Virginia Commonwealth University
Richmond 23284

Washington
University of Washington
Seattle 98195

Washington State University
Pullman 99164

West Virginia
Marshall University
Huntington 25701

West Virginia University
Morgantown 26506

Wisconsin
Marquette University
Milwaukee 53233

University of Wisconsin—Eau Claire
Eau Claire 54701

University of Wisconsin
Madison 53706

University of Wisconsin—Oshkosh
Oshkosh 54901

Wyoming
University of Wyoming
Laramie 82071

APPENDIX D: RÉSUMÉS, APPLICATION FORMS, COVER LETTERS, AND INTERVIEWS

You might see a hurdle to leap over, or a hoop to jump through. Or a barrier to knock down. That is how many people think of résumés, application forms, cover letters, and interviews. But you do not have to think of them that way. They are not ways to keep you from a job; they are ways for you to show an employer what you know and what you can do. After all, you are going to get a job. It is just a question of which one.

Employers want to hire people who can do the job. To learn who these people are, they use résumés, application forms, written tests, performance tests, medical examinations, and interviews. You can use each of these different evaluation procedures to your advantage. You might not be able to make a silk purse out of a sow's ear, but at least you can show what a good ear you have.

CREATING EFFECTIVE RÉSUMÉS AND APPLICATION FORMS

Résumés and application forms are two ways to achieve the same goal: To give the employer written evidence of your qualifications. When creating a résumé or completing an application form, you need two different kinds of information: facts about yourself and facts about the job you want. With this information in hand, you can present the facts about yourself in terms of the job. You have more freedom with a résumé—you can put your best points first and avoid blanks. But, even on application forms, you can describe your qualifications in terms of the job's duties.

Know Thyself

Begin by assembling information about yourself. Some items appear on virtually every résumé or application form, including the following:

- Current address and phone number—if you are rarely at home during business hours, try to give the phone number of a friend or relative who will take messages for you.
- Job sought or career goal
- Experience (paid and volunteer)—date of employment, name and full address of the employer, job title, starting and finishing salary, and reason for leaving (moving, returning to school, and seeking a better position are among the readily accepted reasons).
- Education—the school's name, the city in which it is located, the years you attended it, the diploma or certificate you earned, and the course of studies you pursued.
- Other qualifications—hobbies, organizations you belong to, honors you have received, and leadership positions you have held.
- Office machines, tools, equipment you have used, and skills that you possess.

Other information, such as your Social Security number, is often asked for on application forms but is rarely presented on résumés. Application forms might also ask for a record of past addresses and for information that you would rather not reveal, such as a record of convictions. If asked for such information, you must be honest. Honesty does not, however, require that you reveal disabilities that do not affect your overall qualifications for a job.

Know Thy Job

Next, gather specific information about the jobs you are applying for. You need to know the pay range (so you can make their top your bottom), education and experience usually required, hours and shifts usually worked. Most importantly, you need to know the job duties (so that you can describe your experience in terms of those duties). Study the job description. Some job announcements, especially those issued by a government, even have a checklist that assigns a numerical weight to different qualifications so that you can be certain as to which is the most important; looking at such announcements will give you an idea of what employers look for even if you do not wish to apply for a government job. If the announcement or ad is vague, call the employer to learn what is sought.

Once you have the information you need, you can prepare a résumé. You may need to prepare more than one master résumé if you are going to look for different kinds of jobs. Otherwise, your résumé will not fit the job you seek.

Two Kinds of Résumés   The way you arrange your résumé depends on how well your experience seems to prepare you for the position you want. Basically, you can either describe your most recent job first and work backwards (reverse chronology) or group similar skills together. No matter which format you use, the following advice applies generally.

- Use specifics. A vague description of your duties will make only a vague impression.
- Identify accomplishments. If you headed a project, improved productivity, reduced costs, increased membership, or achieved some other goal, say so.
- Type your résumé, using a standard typeface. (Printed résumés are becoming more common, but employers do not indicate a preference for them.)
- Keep the length down to two pages at the most.
- Remember your mother's advice not to say anything if you cannot say something nice. Leave all embarrassing or negative information off the résumé—but be ready to deal with it in a positive fashion at the interview.
- Proofread the master copy carefully.
- Have someone else proofread the master copy carefully.
- Have a third person proofread the master copy carefully.
- Use the best quality photocopying machine and good white or off-white paper.

The following information appears on almost every résumé.

- Name.
- Phone number at which you can be reached or receive messages.
- Address.
- Job or career sought.
- References—often just a statement that references are available suffices. If your references are likely to be known by the person who reads the résumé, however, their names are worth listing.
- Experience.
- Education.
- Special talents.
- Personal information—height, weight, marital status, physical condition. Although this information appears on virtually every sample résumé I have ever seen, it is not important according to recruiters. In fact, employers are prohibited by law from asking for some of it. If some of this information is directly job related—the height and weight of a bouncer is important to a disco owner, for example—list it. Otherwise, save space and put in more information about your skills.

Reverse chronology is the easiest method to use. It is also the least effective because it makes when you did something more important than what you can do. It is an especially poor format if you have gaps in your work history, if the job you seek is very different from the job you currently hold, or if you are just entering the job market. About the only time you would want to use such a résumé is when you have progressed up a clearly defined career ladder and want to move up a rung.

Résumés that are not chronological may be called functional, analytical, skill oriented, creative, or some other name. The differences are less important than the similarity, which is that all stress what you can do. The advantage to a potential employer—and, therefore, to your job campaign—should be obvious. The employer can see immediately how you will fit the job. This format also has advantages for many job hunters because it camouflages gaps in paid employment and avoids giving prominence to irrelevant jobs.

You begin writing a functional résumé by determining the skills the employer is looking for. Again, study the job description for this information. Next, review your experience and education to see when you demonstrated the ability sought. Then prepare the résumé itself, putting first the information that relates most obviously to the job. The result will be a résumé with headings such as "Engineering," "Computer Languages," "Communications Skills," or "Design Experience." These headings will have much more impact than the dates that you would use on a chronological résumé.

Fit Yourself to a Form

Some large employers, such as fast food restaurants and government agencies, make more use of application forms than of résumés. The forms suit the style of large organizations because people find information more quickly if it always appears in the same place. However, creating a résumé before filling out an application form will still benefit you. You can use the résumé when you send a letter inquiring about a position. You can submit a résumé even if an application is required; it will spotlight your qualifications. And the information on the résumé will serve as a handy reference if you must fill out an application form quickly. Application forms are really just résumés in disguise anyway. No matter how rigid the form appears to be, you can still use it to show why you are the person for the job being filled.

At first glance, application forms seem to give a job hunter no leeway. The forms certainly do not have the flexibility that a résumé does, but you can still use them to your best advantage. Remember that the attitude of the person reading the form is not, "Let's find out why this person is unqualified," but, "Maybe this is the person we want." Use all the parts of the form—experience blocks, education blocks, and others—to show that the person is you.

Here's some general advice on completing application forms.

- Request two copies of the form. If only one is provided, photocopy it before you make a mark on it. You'll need more than one copy to prepare rough drafts.
- Read the whole form before you start completing it.
- Prepare a master copy if the same form is used by several divisions within the same company or organization. Do not put the specific job applied for, date, and signature on the master copy. Fill in that information on the photocopies as you submit them.
- Type the form if possible. If it has lots of little lines that are hard to type within, type the information on a piece of blank paper that will fit in the space, paste the paper over the form, and photocopy the finished product. Such a procedure results in a much neater, easier to read page.
- Leave no blanks; enter n/a (for "not applicable") when the information requested does not apply to you; this tells people checking the form that you did not simply skip the question.
- Carry a résumé and a copy of other frequently asked information (such as previous addresses) with you when visiting potential employers in case you must fill out an application on the spot. Whenever possible, however, fill the form out at home and mail it in with a résumé and a cover letter that point up your strengths.

WRITING INTRIGUING COVER LETTERS

You will need a cover letter whenever you send a résumé or application form to a potential employer. The letter should capture the employer's attention, show why you are writing, indicate why your employment will benefit the company, and ask for an interview. The kind of specific information that must be included in a letter means that each must be written individually. Each letter must also be typed perfectly, which may present a problem. Word processing equipment helps. Frequently only the address, first paragraph, and specifics concerning an interview will vary. These items are easily changed on word processing equipment and memory typewriters. If you do not have access to such equipment, you might be able to rent it. Or you might be able to have your letters typed by a résumé or employment services company listed in the yellow pages. Be sure you know the full cost of such a service before agreeing to use one.

Let's go through a letter point by point.

Salutation

Each letter should be addressed by name to the person you want to talk with. That person is the one who can hire you. This is almost certainly not someone in the personnel department, and it is probably not a department head either. It is most likely to be the person who will actually supervise you once you start work. Call the company to make sure you have the right name. And spell it correctly.

Opening

The opening should appeal to the reader. Cover letters are sales letters. Sales are made after you capture a person's attention. You capture the reader's attention most easily by talking about the company rather than yourself. Mention projects under development, recent awards, or favorable comments recently published about the company. You can find such information in the business press, including the business section of local newspapers and the many magazines that are devoted to particular industries. If you are answering an ad, you may mention it. If someone suggested that you write, use their name (with permission, of course).

Body

The body of the letter gives a brief description of your qualifications and refers to the résumé, where your sales campaign can continue.

Closing

You cannot have what you do not ask for. At the end of the letter, request an interview. Suggest a time and state that you will confirm the appointment. Use a standard complimentary close, such as "Sincerely yours," leave three or four lines for your signature, and type your name. I would type my phone number under my name; this recommendation is not usually made, although phone numbers are found on most letterheads. The alternative is to place the phone number in the body of the letter, but it will be more difficult to find there should the reader wish to call you.

TRIUMPHING ON TESTS AND AT INTERVIEWS

A man with a violin case stood on a subway platform in The Bronx. He asked a conductor, "How do you get to Carnegie Hall?" The conductor replied, "Practice! Practice! Practice!"

Tests

That old joke holds good advice for people preparing for employment tests or interviews. The tests given to job applicants fall into four categories: General aptitude tests, practical tests, tests of physical agility, and medical examinations. You can practice for the first three. If the fourth is required, learn as soon as possible what the disqualifying conditions are, then have your physician examine you for them so that you do not spend years training for a job that you will not be allowed to hold.

To practice for a test, you must learn what the test is. Once again, you must know what job you want to apply for and for whom you want to work in order to find out what tests, if any, are required. Government agencies, which frequently rely on tests, will often provide a sample of the test they use. These samples can be helpful even if an employer uses a different test. Copies of standard government tests are usually available at the library.

If you practice beforehand, you'll be better prepared and less nervous on the day of the test. That will put you ahead of the competition. You will also improve your performance by following this advice:

- Make a list of what you will need at the test center, including a pencil; check it before leaving the house.
- Get a good night's sleep.
- Be at the test center early—at least 15 minutes early.
- Read the instructions carefully; make sure they do not differ from the samples you practiced with.
- Generally, speed counts; do not linger over difficult questions.
- Learn if guessing is penalized. Most tests are scored by counting up the right answers; guessing is all to the good. Some tests are scored by counting the right answers and deducting partial credit for wrong answers; blind guessing will lose you points—but if you can eliminate two wrong choices, a guess might still pay off.

Interviews

For many of us, interviews are the most fearsome part of finding a job. But they are also our best chance to show an employer our qualifications. Interviews are far more flexible than application forms or tests. Use that flexibility to your advantage. As with tests, you can reduce your anxiety and improve your performance by preparing for your interviews ahead of time.

Begin by considering what interviewers want to know. You represent a risk to the employer. A hiring mistake is expensive in terms of lost productivity, wasted training money, and the cost of finding a replacement. To lessen the risk, interviewers try to select people who are highly motivated, understand what the job entails, and show that their background has prepared them for it.

You show that you are highly motivated by learning about the company before the interview, by dressing appropriately, and by being well mannered—which means that you greet the interviewer by name, you do not chew gum or smoke, you listen attentively, and you thank the interviewer at the end of the session. You also show motivation by expressing interest in the job at the end of the interview.

You show that you understand what the job entails and that you can perform it when you explain how your qualifications prepare you for specific duties as described in the company's job listing and when you ask intelligent questions about the nature of the work and the training provided new workers.

One of the best ways to prepare for an interview is to have some practice sessions with a friend or two. Here is a list of some of the most commonly asked questions to get you started.

- Why did you apply for this job?
- What do you know about this job or company?
- Why should I hire you?
- What would you do if . . . (usually filled in with a work-related crisis)?
- How would you describe yourself?
- What would you like to tell me about yourself?
- What are your major strengths?
- What are your major weaknesses?
- What type of work do you like to do best?
- What are your interests outside work?
- What type of work do you like to do least?
- What accomplishment gave you the greatest satisfaction?
- What was your worst mistake?
- What would you change in your past life?
- What courses did you like best or least in school?
- What did you like best or least about your last job?
- Why did you leave your last job?
- Why were you fired?
- How does your education or experience relate to this job?
- What are your goals?
- How do you plan to reach them?
- What do you hope to be doing in 5 years? 10?
- What salary do you expect?

Many jobhunting books available at libraries discuss ways to answer these questions. Essentially, your strategy should be to concentrate on the job and your ability to do it no matter what the question seems to be asking. If asked for a strength, mention something job related. If asked for a weakness, mention a job-related strength (you work too hard, you worry too much about details, you always have to see the big picture). If asked about a disability or a specific negative factor in your past—a criminal record, a failure in school, being fired—be prepared to stress what you learned from the experience, how you have overcome the shortcoming, and how you are now in a position to do a better job.

So far, only the interviewer's questions have been discussed. But an interview will be a two-way conversation. You really do need to learn more about the position to find out if you want the job. Given how frustrating it is to look for a job, you do not want to take just any position only to learn after 2 weeks that you cannot stand the place and have to look for another job right away. Here are some questions for you to ask the interviewer.

- What would a day on this job be like?
- Whom would I report to? May I meet this person?
- Would I supervise anyone? May I meet them?
- How important is this job to the company?
- What training programs are offered?
- What advancement opportunities are offered?
- Why did the last person leave this job?
- What is that person doing now?
- What is the greatest challenge of this position? What plans does the company have with regard to...? (Mention some development of which you have read or heard.)
- Is the company growing?

After you ask such questions, listen to the interviewer's answers and then, if at all possible, point to something in your education or experience related to it. You might notice that questions about salary and fringe benefits are not included in the above list. Your focus at a first interview should be the company and what you will do for it, not what it will pay you. The salary range will often be given in the ad or position announcement, and information on the usual fringe benefits will be available from the personnel department. Once you have been offered a position, you can negotiate the salary. The jobhunting guides available in bookstores and at the library give many more hints on this subject.

At the end of the interview, you should know what the next step will be: Whether you should contact the interviewer again, whether you should provide more information, whether more interviews must be conducted, and when a final decision will be reached. Try to end on a positive note by reaffirming your interest in the position and pointing out why you will be a good choice to fill it.

Immediately after the interview, make notes of what went well and what you would like to improve. To show your interest in the position, send a followup letter to the interviewer, providing further information on some point raised in the interview and thanking the interviewer once again. Remember, someone is going to hire you; it might be the person you just talked to.

This appendix is reprinted from *Occupational Outlook Quarterly,* spring 1987, volume 31, number 1, pp. 17–23.

Chronological Résumé

Allison Springs
15 Hilton House
College de l'Art Libre
Smallville, CO 77717

(888) 736-3550

Job sought: Food Industry Sales Representative

Education

September 1984 to June 1988	College de l'Art Libre College Lane Smallville, CO 77717	Vice President, Junior Class (raised $15,000 for junior project) Member College Service Club (2 years) Swim Team (4 years) Harvest Celebration Director Major: Political science with courses in economics and accounting

Experience

Period employed	Employer	Job title and duties
January 1988 to present 10 hours per week	McCall, McCrow, and McCow 980 Main Street Westrow, CO 77718 Supervisor: Jan Eagelli	Research assistant: Conducted research on legal and other matters for members of the firm.
September 1987 to December 1987 10 hours per week	Department of Public Assistance State of Colorado 226 Park Street Smallville, CO 77717 Supervisor: James Fish	Claims interviewer: Interviewed clients to determine their eligibility for various assistance programs. Directed them to special administrators when appropriate.
Summers 1981-1986	Shilo Pool 46 Waterway Shilo, NE 77777 Supervisor: Leander Neptune	Lifeguard: Insured safety of patrons by seeing that rules were obeyed, testing chemical content of the water, and inspecting mechanical equipment.

Recommendations available on request

Functional Résumé

Allison Springs
15 Hilton House
College de l'Art Libre
Smallville, CO 77717

(888) 736-3550

Job sought: Food Industry Sales Representative

Skills, education, and experience

Negotiating skills: My participation in student government has developed my negotiating skills, enabling me both to persuade others of the advantages to them of a different position and to reach a compromise between people who wish to pursue different goals.

Promotional skills: The effective use of posters, displays, and other visual aids contributed greatly to my successful campaign for class office (Junior Class Vice President), committee projects, and fund raising efforts (which netted $15,000 for the junior class project).

Skill working with people: All the jobs I have had involve working closely with people on many different levels. As Vice President of the Junior Class, I balanced the concerns of different groups in order to reach a common goal. As a claims interviewer with a state public assistance agency, I dealt with people under very trying circumstances. As a research assistant with a law firm, I worked with both lawyers and clerical workers. And as a lifeguard (5 summers), I learned how to manage groups. In addition, my work with the state and the law office has made me familiar with organizational procedures.

Chronology

September 1984 to present	Attended College de l'Art Libre in Smallville, Colorado. Will earn a Bachelor of Arts degree in political science. Elected Vice President of the Junior Class, managed successful fund drive, directed Harvest Celebration Committee, served on many other committees, and earned 33 percent of my college expenses.
January 1988 to present	Work as research assistant for the law office of McCall, McCrow, and McCow, 980 Main Street, Westrow, Colorado 77718. Supervisor: Jan Eagelli (666) 654-3211
September 1987 to December 1987	Served as claims interviewer intern for the Department of Public Assistance of the State of Colorado, 226 Park Street, Smallville, Colorado 77717. Supervisor: James Fish (666) 777-7717.
1981-1986	Worked as lifeguard during the summer at the Shilo Pool, 46 Waterway, Shilo, Nebraska 77777.

Recommendations available on request

Cover Letter

15 Hilton House
College de l'Art Libre
Smallville, CO 77717
March 18, 1988

Ms. Collette Recruiter
Rest Easy Hotels
1500 Suite Street
Megapolis, SD 99999

Dear Ms. Recruiter:

The Rest Easy Hotels always served as landmarks for me when I traveled through this country and Europe. I would like to contribute to their growth, especially their new chain, the Suite Rest Hotels that feature reception rooms for every guest. I have had many jobs working with people and have always enjoyed this aspect of my experience. Knowing its importance to your company, I believe I would be an asset to the Rest Easy Hotels.

During the week of March 31, I will be visiting Megapolis and would like to speak with you concerning your training program for hotel managers. I will call your secretary to confirm an appointment.

The enclosed résumé outlines my education and experience.

Sincerely yours,

Allison Springs

Allison Springs
(888) 736-3550

VGM CAREER BOOKS

OPPORTUNITIES IN
*Available in both paperback and
   hardbound editions*

Accounting Careers
Acting Careers
Advertising Careers
Aerospace Careers
Agriculture Careers
Airline Careers
Animal and Pet Care
Appraising Valuation Science
Architecture
Automotive Service
Banking
Beauty Culture
Biological Sciences
Biotechnology Careers
Book Publishing Careers
Broadcasting Careers
Building Construction Trades
Business Communication Careers
Business Management
Cable Television
Carpentry Careers
Chemical Engineering
Chemistry Careers
Child Care Careers
Chiropractic Health Care
Civil Engineering Careers
Commercial Art and Graphic Design
Computer Aided Design and Computer
   Aided Mfg.
Computer Maintenance Careers
Computer Science Careers
Counseling & Development
Crafts Careers
Culinary Careers
Dance
Data Processing Careers
Dental Care
Drafting Careers
Electrical Trades
Electronic and Electrical Engineering
Energy Careers
Engineering Careers
Engineering Technology Careers
Environmental Careers
Eye Care Careers
Fashion Careers
Fast Food Careers
Federal Government Careers
Film Careers
Financial Careers
Fire Protection Services
Fitness Careers
Food Services
Foreign Language Careers
Forestry Careers
Gerontology Careers
Government Service
Graphic Communications
Health and Medical Careers
High Tech Careers
Home Economics Careers
Hospital Administration
Hotel & Motel Management
Human Resources Management Careers

Industrial Design
Information Systems Careers
Insurance Careers
Interior Design
International Business
Journalism Careers
Landscape Architecture
Laser Technology
Law Careers
Law Enforcement and Criminal Justice
Library and Information Science
Machine Trades
Magazine Publishing Careers
Management
Marine & Maritime Careers
Marketing Careers
Materials Science
Mechanical Engineering
Medical Technology Careers
Microelectronics
Military Careers
Modeling Careers
Music Careers
Newspaper Publishing Careers
Nursing Careers
Nutrition Careers
Occupational Therapy Careers
Office Occupations
Opticianry
Optometry
Packaging Science
Paralegal Careers
Paramedical Careers
Part-time & Summer Jobs
Performing Arts Careers
Petroleum Careers
Pharmacy Careers
Photography
Physical Therapy Careers
Physician Careers
Plumbing & Pipe Fitting
Podiatric Medicine
Printing Careers
Property Management Careers
Psychiatry
Psychology
Public Health Careers
Public Relations Careers
Purchasing Careers
Real Estate
Recreation and Leisure
Refrigeration and Air Conditioning
   Trades
Religious Service
Restaurant Careers
Retailing
Robotics Careers
Sales Careers
Sales & Marketing
Secretarial Careers
Securities Industry
Social Science Careers
Social Work Careers
Speech-Language Pathology Careers
Sports & Athletics
Sports Medicine
State and Local Government

Teaching Careers
Technical Communications
Telecommunications
Television and Video Careers
Theatrical Design & Production
Transportation Careers
Travel Careers
Veterinary Medicine Careers
Vocational and Technical Careers
Welding Careers
Word Processing
Writing Careers
Your Own Service Business

CAREERS IN
Accounting
Advertising
Business
Communications
Computers
Education
Engineering
Health Care
Science

CAREER DIRECTORIES
Careers Encyclopedia
Occupational Outlook Handbook

CAREER PLANNING
Admissions Guide to Selective
   Business Schools
Career Planning and Development for
   College Students and Recent Graduates
Careers Checklists
Careers for Bookworms and
   Other Literary Types
Careers for Sports Nuts
Handbook of Business and
   Management Careers
Handbook of Scientific and
   Technical Careers
How to Change Your Career
How to Get and Get Ahead
   On Your First Job
How to Get People to Do Things Your
   Way
How to Have a Winning Job Interview
How to Land a Better Job
How to Make the Right Career Moves
How to Prepare for College
How to Run Your Own Home Business
How to Write a Winning Résumé
Joyce Lain Kennedy's Career Book
Life Plan
Planning Your Career of Tomorrow
Planning Your College Education
Planning Your Military Career
Planning Your Young Child's Education

SURVIVAL GUIDES
Dropping Out or Hanging In
High School Survival Guide
College Survival Guide

VGM Career Horizons
A Division of National Textbook Company
4255 West Touhy Avenue
Lincolnwood, Illinois 60646-1975 U.S.A.